Not Just Polio

My Life Story

RICHARD LLOYD DAGGETT

iUniverse, Inc.
New York   Bloomington

iUniverse books may be ordered through booksellers or by contacting:

iUniverse
1663 Liberty Drive
Bloomington, IN 47403
www.iuniverse.com
1-800-Authors (1-800-288-4677)

Because of the dynamic nature of the Internet, any Web addresses or links contained in this book may have changed since publication and may no longer be valid. The views expressed in this work are solely those of the author and do not necessarily reflect the views of the publisher, and the publisher hereby disclaims any responsibility for them.

ISBN: 978-1-4401-9815-1 (sc)
ISBN: 978-1-4401-9816-8 (ebook)
ISBN: 978-1-4401-9817-5 (hc)

Printed in the United States of America

iUniverse rev. date: 04/28/2010

To my parents, Norma and Rodney Daggett, Sr., for giving me the gift of a remarkably full and enjoyable life.

To my sister, Ann, and my brothers, Rodney and Robert, for always being there.

To Mary Clarke Atwood, for being my writing buddy.

To Janice Flood Nichols, for writing *Twin Voices*, an excellent retelling of the polio experience. It was reading *Twin Voices* that helped in my decision to publish this review of my life.

To the staff of Rancho Los Amigos National Rehabilitation Center, for providing the best possible care to polio patients and others with disabling conditions.

It's not what life holds that counts, it's what you bring to it.

Contents

Proceeds from the sale of this book will be divided between The Amigos Fund of Rancho Los Amigos National Rehabilitation Center and the Polio Survivors Association.

Foreword

Richard Daggett's autobiography presents a clear and comprehensive view of his experience with polio. Every episode he reviews is stimulating and told with candor. His ability to attain the equivalent of a college education, despite being physically unable to enter the classroom, is a subtle but strong display of his strength. The vision and determination which became evident during this long challenge were, without a doubt, significant elements which enhanced his effectiveness as an advocate to improve the welfare, comfort, and safety of the severely disabled patients who lacked adequate resources.

Several distinct events impacted Richard's polio involvement. They display the challenges faced by the medical services in Los Angeles County, as the clinicians responded to the dynamic changes presented by modern poliomyelitis epidemics.

Historically, poliomyelitis was an ancient, highly contagious yet mildly paralytic disease. It appeared as an occasional summer epidemic. Richard, and the other residents of Los Angeles County, had a very different experience. The rapid population growth during the decade that followed World War II, combined with the temperate climate of southern California, replaced a manageable disease with massive and prolonged epidemics. The patient census quadrupled— sixteen hundred per year versus four hundred per year—and the paralytic intensity increased.

The experience of impending respiratory failure adds considerable anxiety to the patient's physical distress. When a patient was admitted to the Los Angeles County communicable disease ward, the admitting doctors promptly followed their motto for judging the level of acute care needed. This motto was, "If the thought of a tracheotomy enters your mind, *do it now.*" This procedure gave the physician direct access to the lungs and assured a clear airway. The rate of survival increased to 95 percent. Richard had his tracheotomy as the first step in his care.

Since community hospitals lacked the facilities and staff to manage severe respiratory paralysis, a special medical unit with the additional staff was established at what had been the Rancho Los Amigos Poor Farm. A representative team from the National Foundation for Infantile Paralysis evaluated Rancho's original program and found more warehousing than modern therapy. The Foundation recommended upgrading to a Regional Respiratory Center and offered selected support by the March of Dimes. The local authorities agreed to provide a new building and more staff. Dr. John Affeldt, the consulting pulmonary specialist, accepted the invitation to direct the new center. Richard, unable to move his limbs, swallow, or breathe on his own, was transferred to this modern facility as soon as his contagion subsided.

Dr Affeldt, as director of the unit, also had concern for loss of limb and spine function and, especially, the patient's inability to sit erect. He recruited an orthopedic surgeon and former classmate to assume the task of finding a solution. Dr. Vernon Nickel agreed to come to Rancho, but because of his busy private practice, he would need help to accomplish this goal. His brother, Eldon Nickel, also a physician, recommended one of his classmates who was just finishing a residency in orthopedic surgery and not inclined to open a private practice. I was that person. I was pleased to join the orthopedic staff at Rancho in July 1955, and my involvement continues.

It quickly became apparent that the severely paralyzed spines of our polio patients were not adequately stabilized, even with the use of plaster body jackets. Also, these body jackets restricted chest expansion, often inhibiting already compromised pulmonary function. Recovering the patient's erect posture would require an extensive surgical fusion, yet our patients' ability to breathe was limited. Prior experience with emergency surgeries for kidney stones or pregnancies had demonstrated that a tracheotomy could provide safe and effective anesthesia for patients with a vital capacity less than 60 percent normal.

The unknown factor was the necessary length of a fusion. Traditional spine fusions to correct a deformed column only involved the dominant, primary curve. This proved to be inadequate for the spine paralyzed by polio. The tilted vertabrae continued to bend around each end of the fusion. In contrast, the vertebrae with muscle control and their intervertebral spaces are horizontal. Hence, the rule for the fusion of a paretic spine is to include all tilted vertebrae, extending each end of the fusion into the first two horizontal vertebrae.

During his first two years at Rancho, Richard recovered independent breathing and leg strength sufficient for walking with braces. His spine, however, showed no significant gains. In fact, asymmetric weakness of his trunk muscles was creating an early scoliosis. Dr. Vernon Nickel and I successfully stabilized Richard's spine, and this spinal fusion has allowed him to sit and stand erect.

Rancho Los Amigos was also a pioneer in home health for those with severe disability. We could do much to improve the patients' function, but it would not be of benefit if these patients remained confined to the hospital. Rancho led the way with mechanical home ventilation and provided a support structure to ensure success. This support included a special team of technicians, called the Medical Equipment Repair Service, who went to the homes of out-patients to maintain respirators—including iron lungs and other life support equipment. Rancho even supplied our respirator-dependent patients with backup electric generators. Patients with very severe polio residuals were able to return home, once again entering family life and contributing to society.

The scourge of acute polio was rapidly eliminated in the western world by Dr. Jonas Salk's antiviral vaccine. At Rancho, the wards did not empty as rapidly, but within three to five years the staff was free to turn the skills they had perfected with polio towards other severely disabled patients.

Attention mainly focused on two clinical groups at Los Angeles County General Hospital—spinal cord injury and stroke. As with early polio, available care had been warehousing more than therapeutic. The rules for rehabilitation had yet to be determined. A separate unit was established at Rancho for each of these clinical groups, and team treatment was initiated. Common to both was the need to correct, minimize, and prevent the ill effects of prolonged bed rest, including contractures and pressure sores. Research projects were organized to factually define the functional differences between polio, spinal cord injury, and stroke. Rancho continues to remain at the forefront of innovation in the care of persons with severe paralysis.

Jacquelin Perry, MD
Emeritus Chief , Polio and Gait Clinic and Pathokinesiology Program at
Rancho Los Amigos
Professor Emeritus, Department of Orthopaedics
at the University of Southern California Keck School of Medicine

Introduction

I started writing the story of my life in 1990. I was writing a family history and found the handwritten notes I had made when I was a patient at Rancho Los Amigos Hospital. These notes were used as a starting point for this review of my life.

Over the next few years, I would occasionally bring this document up on the computer screen and add a paragraph or two. I didn't write much because I was too involved with other writing tasks. About ten years after my initial entries I began to work seriously on my story. I wanted it to include more than my polio experiences. Polio certainly had a major impact on my life, but polio is not my only life. That is why I chose *Not Just Polio* as my title.

It was surprisingly easy to add memories of my childhood. One episode would instantly lead to a recollection of another. I had little difficulty reliving those early years. The bigger problem was trying to stop writing. Memories flooded my mind. I was blessed with a happy childhood and a caring, supportive family. I hope my narrative gives evidence of this.

A computer certainly makes writing a life review easier. You can write about something that happened at any point in time, and then copy and paste it to where it makes sense in the context of your story. I decided to keep my story in chronological order as much as possible. It was easier for me to think about my life in this way.

Yet, when I was proofing my story, I realized there were parts, even in separate paragraphs, that read like one very long, run-on sentence. I decided to put visual breaks at strategic points to indicate where one thought or incident ended and another began.

A few friends and professional colleagues reviewed my rough draft. All of them felt it was a worthwhile endeavor. Most urged me to add more about my personal experiences and feelings, especially during my polio hospitalization.

One of my colleagues really pushed me on this. He said he'd never read anything that told this type of story from a teenager's perspective. There have been several books that look back on a younger child's polio experiences, and a few that relate the story of an adult like Franklin Roosevelt, but none that he knew of that explored severe disability and lengthy hospitalization from a teenager's viewpoint. He also wanted me to include more about how disability affected my adult life.

He reminded me that, for several years, I had made myself available to first-year medical students from the University of Southern California. I was part of a team of adults with disabilities that the students visited to improve their interview skills. They asked us about our disabilities and our medical histories. I always told them that no questions were off-limits. Some of the students asked insightful questions about the impact of physical limitations on my personal life. I answered truthfully and with as much detail as was necessary. It didn't embarrass me at all. My colleague knew this, and encouraged me to be just as open in this life review.

I still wasn't sure I wanted to put my very personal thoughts and experiences in writing for all the world to see. My story was put away for a few years while I gave this more thought. Eventually, more paragraphs were written and rewritten as I tried to find some middle ground. I wasn't willing to "tell all," but I wanted my story to be more than dates and places. Following my colleague's urgings, I added more of my thoughts, and more detail about my personal experiences. I apologize if my references to personal details and biological processes offend anyone.

Also, in the last few years, I have heard some people say that the polio vaccine is no longer needed, or that all vaccines are bad and cause more harm than good. With religious zeal they condemn drug companies, our government, and the medical establishment. Facts don't seem to faze them. They continue to preach bad medicine and are sometimes successful in clouding the minds of parents.

Vaccines have nearly eliminated polio and have actually eliminated smallpox. What a gift to mankind! This gift is not recognized by the anti-vaccination lobby. They have benefited from this gift because other, more enlightened people have accepted the gift. The vaccine opponents have been given a free ride. They are free of smallpox and polio, because other people have done the responsible thing and gotten vaccinated.

If retelling my polio story helps even one undecided parent get their child immunized, then writing my story has been worthwhile. In 1953, the year I contracted polio, there were approximately 32,000 documented cases of polio in the United States, and more American children died of polio than of any other communicable disease. The year before there were more than 58,000 documented cases of polio in the United States. Just imagine how many hospital wards we would need now, more than fifty years later, if there had been no vaccine. Polio is still endemic in parts of the world. We are all, infants and adults, just one airplane flight away from this scourge. Some people might think they are safe because it is, "over there." But one person traveling "over there" can quickly bring it over here.

It would also please me if my story inspired you to write about *your* life. A person doesn't have to do great deeds to have an interesting life. Everyone has a story to tell. Your friends will enjoy reading it, and your children and grandchildren will appreciate it.

My Early Years

I've always enjoyed poems, those childhood rhymes that most children were taught when I was young. I especially liked the works of Robert Louis Stevenson. We had an early edition of *A Child's Garden of Verses,* and my parents read to me as I looked at the illustrations. Later, probably by the age of eight or nine, I discovered the difference between poems and poetry. My ears would perk up if I heard someone reading something by Robert Frost. One of my favorites is Frost's "The Road Not Taken." It ends with:

> Two roads diverged in a wood, and I—
> I took the one less traveled by,
> And that has made all the difference.

I liked that thought—taking the road less traveled. A psychologist might analyze my feelings and presume that this is based on the fact that my life has been different. This analysis might be right. I've certainly taken the road less traveled, even if the decision was not entirely my own. Circumstances surely had a role in which road I took.

Then, recently, a new book of poetry was given to me. In it was "The Road Not Taken." As I read it again, savoring the flow of Frost's words, my thoughts were suddenly interrupted. It was as if my brain yelled, "Hey! Wait a minute!" I re-read the last two lines:

I took the one less traveled by,
And that has made all the difference.

The questioning part of my brain exerted itself and seemed to ask, "How could a person know if one road, 'made all the difference' without traveling both roads?"

Mrs. Truxaw, my sixth grade teacher, taught her students to read with a critical eye. She urged us to decide for ourselves if an author's words spoke truth to us. I guess I'll have to blame her for my skepticism.

But, as my mother would probably say, I'm getting ahead of myself. I guess I'd better start from the beginning.

I was born on June 14, 1940, at Queen of Angels Hospital in Los Angeles, California, and was the last of my parents' four children. My brother Robert is three years older, my sister Ann is eight years older, and my brother Rodney Jr. is almost exactly ten years older.

Let me provide some historical background, to put my story in context. June 14 is Flag Day in the United States. On June 14, 1940, the German army entered Paris and, on the same day, a group of 728 Polish prisoners became the first residents of the Auschwitz concentration camp. A few days before this, the British Expeditionary Force had been evacuated from Dunkirk and Winston Churchill had addressed the British Parliament, saying, "We shall defend our Island, whatever the cost may be, we shall fight on the beaches, we shall fight on the landing grounds, we shall fight in the fields and in the streets, we shall fight in the hills; we shall never surrender."

Across the Atlantic, the United States was attempting to stay out of this new war. The top recordings of that year were, "In The Mood" by Glenn Miller, "I'll Never Smile Again" by Tommy Dorsey, with the vocal by Frank Sinatra, and "When You Wish Upon a Star" from the Disney movie *Pinocchio*, with the vocal by Cliff Edwards.

The highest rated movies of 1940 included *The Grapes of Wrath*, *The Philadelphia Story*, and *Pinocchio*.

When I was born our family lived at 411 East 109th Street. This was my home for the first ten years of my life. My father and grandfather had built our house themselves in 1932, with some of the plumbing and electrical work contracted out to my father's friends. This was during the Great Depression, and those friends needed work.

The neighborhood consisted of modest, middle-class homes and ours was the largest and nicest on the block. I believe it was the only two-story house. We had a sort of Daggett family compound, since my father and my grandfather owned four adjoining lots. Our house was built on the easternmost lot. Aunt Evelyn's house was next to ours and my grandparents had the house next to her. The remaining lot was vacant, except for my grandfather's garage and workshop.

Our lot was not big, but as a child it seemed big to me. In the beginning, the front lawn sloped gently toward the sidewalk. In 1945, my father added a low cement retaining wall that leveled off the lawn. Aunt Evelyn did the same thing. They probably did it for aesthetic reasons but to us kids it made a much nicer, flat area to play outdoor games. I used the low retaining wall as my "launching pad" when I was learning to ride a full-size bicycle. I would stand on the wall and swing one leg over the bicycle seat, keeping one foot firmly on the wall. When I felt steady, I would propel myself forward.

Our backyard was divided by a low picket fence. The part nearer to the house was planted in grass and flowers, and beyond the fence was what we called "the way back." It was mostly bare ground with colorful shrubs around the perimeter. During World War II we had a Victory Garden in this part of the yard, and after the war my father built a large swing in this area. At the end of the yard we had a covered area with a picnic table and large brick barbecue. Behind the garage we had a chicken yard, although the chickens were gone by the time I was five years old. I remember my father cutting the head off a chicken. It ran around in crazy circles, splattering blood on Aunt Evelyn's garage. After the chickens were gone, my brother Robert and I used the empty walk-in chicken coop for our club house. Between the garage and the chicken coop was a small, L-shaped building we called the wood shed. The lawn mower, garden tools, and some lumber and plumbing supplies were kept there. It was usually dark and, as a young boy, it seemed spooky to me. I hated to walk in there and get tangled in spider webs. When I was older, we built secret panels between the club house, the wood shed, and the space between the garage and our neighbor's yard. We probably got the idea for secret panels from watching so many Saturday afternoon movie serials.

My father built a small room in the attic of the garage. He called this his "dog house" and I think it probably served as his refuge from four active kids. Access was by steep, narrow stairs with a right angle turn halfway up. He had a desk and his self-made photo enlarger in the room. On the desk was a typewriter. Before I could spell or read I would sit at the desk and "type." I would type three to five letters and make a space, then three to five more letters, continuing all the way across the page. When I finished a line I'd move the carriage to the beginning of the line and type over my first letters, each time making sure to use a different letter. The first time I did this my father looked at me and asked, "Just what are you doing?" I told him I was typing Chinese.

The room had a padlock on the door and was off-limits unless we were invited. Of course, anything that is off-limits to a child is a tempting target. There was one small window in the gable end of the garage that provided light and fresh air to this small room, and a portion of one inside wall was hinged and could be swung open to provide the room with cross ventilation. When I was eight, I found a way to climb up on the garage roof trusses and work my way into the room through this hinged portion of the wall. There wasn't much up there that was of interest to a child, but getting inside was a goal in itself.

One of my earliest recollections is of my father building our backyard swing. He put a single, large pipe in the ground. The top of the pipe was over eight feet high. At the top of this pipe he fitted another large pipe going horizontally, with the other end attached to the roof of the wood shed. The swing hung from this pipe. It was the largest backyard swing I can recall ever seeing. I was getting over some childhood illness when he was working on the swing, so my mother let me sit outside and watch him. I remember sitting in an old wooden highchair that all of us kids used when we were small.

I also remember walking around the house on my sister's feet. She would hold my arms up, I would put my feet on top of hers, and I would walk backward as she walked forward. Once we walked all the way to the Diamond Market this way.

The Diamond Market was just north of the corner of 109th Street and Avalon. It was an old-fashioned market, with the front open to the sidewalk. All of the fruits and vegetables were displayed in large bins with metal wheels. A canvas awning rolled out to cover the area. When the market was closed, the bins were pushed back into the building, the awning was retracted, and large sliding doors were closed to secure the building. This left an extra-wide concrete sidewalk that we used for roller skating.

A block north of the market was a small variety store called Martha's. I enjoyed going inside and looking at the toys and games. It rivaled the Sears catalog as my favorite "wish" place.

We had a Sears Silverstone combination 78-rpm record player and radio. It was in a large, wood-veneer console that was part of the living room furniture. The record player also had the capability of making our own records. Not tape recordings or wire recordings, but actual 78 rpm records. One Christmas, the microphone was passed around the room for each person to say something or perform. Ann sang "Away in the Manger," but the only thing they got out of me was a very faint, "Hello, Mommy!"

We had a collection of classical records that I called "the oatmeal records" because of the color of the album cover. Robert and I would play Rossini's "William Tell Overture," and when the "Lone Ranger" theme would start, we would run around and around from the living room, down the hall, into the kitchen, through the breakfast room, through the dining room, and back to the living room. There were also selections by Grieg, Tchaikovsky, and others. We had another album with Prokofiev's *Peter and the Wolf,* narrated by Basil Rathbone. I've heard many later versions of this classic narrated by other people, but in my opinion none of them compare to this version. We weren't force-fed classical music, but it was always a part of our environment.

I remember a time at school when our music teacher played some familiar excerpts of classical music on the record player. She asked the pupils to raise their hands if they could identify the music. One piece she played was the "William Tell Overture." Almost every pupil raised their hand. In unison they shouted, "The Lone Ranger music!" One girl and I were the only ones to offer the correct name.

At home we also had access to a variety of books and magazines that helped in our education. There were always reference books, dictionaries, and encyclopedias in the house, and my parents always encouraged us to, "Look it up." My parents subscribed to *National Geographic* and several art and literature publications. We visited our local library often. Even before I could read, I would sit on the floor in the children's section and leaf through the books with pictures.

∮ ∮ ∮ ∮ ∮

My father worked for Western Electric, a division of AT&T. He was an installation supervisor, managing the installation of communication equipment at large telephone offices and many major aerospace corporations. My mother was a stay-at-home mom, although she was active outside the home in church, the PTA, and other civic and cultural organizations.

My mother was a wonderful cook, and I enjoyed watching her cook and bake. As I grew older I often helped prepare simple meals. There was very little candy or junk food in the house. The closest I came to eating junk food was when I'd make a peanut butter and brown sugar sandwich.

When I was young, my mother would often fix a special breakfast treat for me. She called it a "smashed egg." It was a freshly hardboiled egg that she mashed with a fork, then added a very small amount of salt, pepper, and butter. In the summer months I'd usually have cold cereal and in the winter months I'd have hot Wheatena cereal or sometimes hot oatmeal with raisins.

A lot of kids balk at eating foods like spinach or Brussels sprouts, but I never did. Like most people, I have some favorite foods, but there are not many foods that I really dislike. However, my mother served beef tongue for supper once when I was a child and I protested very strongly. I think it was more the look of it rather than the taste. Maybe if my mother hadn't told me what it was, it would have gone down easier. Mushrooms and shellfish round out my list of least favorite foods. Most other foods, including all types of vegetables, are part of my regular diet. Even as a child I had a small garden patch at the side of our garage. I grew spinach, radishes, and rhubarb.

If I had an upset stomach, my mother would give me sips of 7-Up, and if I was recovering from severe nausea, she would make non-alcoholic eggnog. She said these drinks would make me feel better. They probably did, but I can't think of either one now without their association with feeling ill.

＠＠＠＠＠

In 1946, my father converted the unfinished second story of our house into rooms for us boys. My brother Rodney had a bedroom facing east, Robert and I shared a bedroom facing west, and there was a multi-purpose playroom facing north. That room had a large window that could be opened like a door and led out onto the patio roof. We would sometimes go out onto the roof to watch the Fourth of July fireworks. We could see the aerial rocket display above the Los Angeles Coliseum.

My brother Robert would sometimes jump from this roof to the lawn below. I wanted to, but I always chickened out when I got close to the edge. One time, when I was standing on the edge trying to get up the courage to jump, he came up behind me and said, "Pretend I'm a Jap and I'm going to stab you with my bayonet." World War II was still a vivid memory. He started yelling and making menacing faces as he came closer. My imagination overcame my fear of jumping and I leaped off the roof. I landed on the lawn, turned around, and looked up toward Robert still standing on the roof. It hadn't been as difficult as I had expected. I ran back in the house, up the stairs, out onto the patio roof, and jumped again.

＠＠＠＠＠

About twice a year I would go with my mother to downtown Los Angeles. We would walk from our home near the corner of 109th and Avalon to the streetcar stop at 108th and Broadway. I would tag along as she shopped at the large department stores. Sometimes we would stop at the Red Goose Bootery to buy me a pair of shoes. The store had a kind of fluoroscope that would give a view of a child's bone structure inside a pair of shoes. The child would stand on a shelf, with his feet sticking in an opening, and the shoe salesman would look at the child's feet through a viewing screen. I would often ask to wear the new shoes on the way home, but I usually regretted it by the time we got back to the house. The distance from the streetcar stop at 108th and Broadway to our house doesn't seem very far now, but I remember it as quite a hike for a small child in new shoes.

When I was a child I often wore a sport coat and bow tie to church or special occasions. I enjoyed wearing nice clothes. Once, when I was twelve, I went to a Saturday afternoon movie with one of my friends. I wore a clean white shirt and dress slacks. My friend came out of his house in old Levis and a shirt that had been worn for several days. His mother looked at me and made him change into something better. He didn't like doing that, and said to me, "Why do you always have to wear your good clothes when we go places?" I didn't have a ready answer for him. I just thought it looked better.

6⌒   6⌒   6⌒   6⌒   6⌒

Like my brothers and sister, I had chores to do. I don't remember them as very much of a burden. My mother would sometimes ask my brother Robert and me to wax the linoleum in the kitchen and breakfast room. Robert would smear a coat of wax on a wide area, and then we would polish it by sliding across the floor in our stocking feet. I took my turn drying the dishes and I took out the garbage. This was before the days of garbage disposals. The garbage pails were out in "the way back," near the incinerator. When I was small this bothered me if I had to take the garbage out after dark. The walk to the incinerator was not a problem, but my mind would sometimes play tricks on me as I returned toward the house. I could imagine things lurking in the shadows. I would often be running as I returned to the back door.

I was also designated to take newspapers to an elderly lady who lived a couple of blocks north of us. Mrs. Lovess lived alone and my parents would save our newspapers for her. Every few days I would carry a bundle of them to her house. My mother had several older ladies as friends. I think she met most of them through various adult school classes she attended. They probably weren't that old, but when you are a child everybody older than your parents seems old.

Another "chore" would be mixing the coloring into the margarine. In the 1940s there was some sort of law or regulation that said stores couldn't sell margarine that looked like butter. The coloring had to be added after the customer purchased it. My mother bought margarine in a plastic pouch. The coloring was in a small capsule within the pouch. You'd pinch the capsule to break it, and then knead the pouch to mix the coloring into the margarine. Robert and I would sometimes play catch with the pouch as a way of kneading it. Once we got a little overenthusiastic, and hit the ceiling with the pouch. It split, leaving a quarter-size spot of margarine on the dining room ceiling. The stain was still on the ceiling when we sold the house and moved to Downey.

On Christmas mornings, Robert and I would usually be the first ones up. For some reason Robert would tell me that it was OK for me to come to the living room, but he wouldn't let me see the Christmas tree with the presents underneath until the rest of the family got up. I had to put my hands over my eyes and he would lead me through the house. Once, when I was about five or six, he had me lie down on the sofa and he covered me, head and all, with a crocheted afghan my mother had made. I felt I had really fooled him. I could see right through the afghan's open mesh.

Robert and I often massaged each other's back. We called it "tickling" the back. We would take turns lying face down on the sofa, with our shirt lifted, and have kitchen or household items rubbed across our back. We would use a basting brush, door keys, a bottle opener, or something similar, and try to identify the object. Sometimes we would spell words with our finger and the person lying down would try to "read" the word. I still enjoy having my back rubbed.

I don't remember my parents being overly strict, or scolding us often, but they expected certain standards of behavior. They expected us to be polite and show respect to others. We were taught to use proper grammar and were promptly corrected if we erred. I'm sure this helped me later in reading and English classes. Swearing was forbidden, although I never had my mouth washed out with soap. It was just understood that swearing was not allowed. I remember in the early 1950s when my sister bought a used 1946 Chevy coupe. It was "nosed" and "decked." When she pulled in the driveway I said, "Bitchin'," current slang for something really nice. My mother was standing a few feet away and gave me a look that indicated strong disapproval. It was the kind of look that only a mother can give.

Another thing that was forbidden was alcohol. My mother was just one degree away from being a complete teetotaler. She would have brandy available for fruit cake, or occasionally some flavored liqueur if a recipe required it, but that was about it. The only exception was sometimes at Thanksgiving or Easter she might serve the adults a small glass of Manischewitz Concord Grape wine. After we kids were grown she loosened up a little, but just a little. If my parents and I were at an upscale Mexican restaurant, she might be tempted to order a margarita. Even then she couldn't quite escape her previous constraints. She wouldn't order a drink for herself but would say to my father, "If you'd like a margarita I'll split it with you."

Once I came close to causing a real disaster. Richard Lundy brought over a pack of cigarettes when we were about seven. We went into our chicken coop clubhouse to try smoking. They tasted awful, but we thought we were acting really grown up. There was an old mattress leaning against the wall, waiting to be taken to the dump, and there was also a box with some old crepe-paper decorations on the floor. I touched the end of my lighted cigarette to a piece of crepe-paper. It ignited immediately, almost explosively, and spread to the underside of the mattress. We tried to put it out by stomping on it, but the flames were getting ahead of us. My parents were at the market, but luckily my brother Rodney was home. We yelled and he came running out the back door, grabbed the garden hose, and doused the flames. There was no damage to the chicken coop, but the crepe-paper was just a pile of ash and the underside of the mattress was gone. Richard and I knew we were in real trouble, so we made a deal. I would tell my parents that it was his fault, and he would tell his parents that it was mine.

On 109th Street we had several neighbor families with children about my age. The Elwood boys lived six houses east of us, the Lundy family lived four houses east, and the Nielsons lived west of us, in the house that my grandparents built.

The Lundys had two children. Richard was about my age, and Ruth Ann was a couple of years younger. Everybody called her "Sissy," probably because her brother had trouble saying "sister" when he was young. The Nielson boys were Johnny and Donald. Johnny was two years older, and Donald was two years my junior. My cousins, Arthur, Dick, and Raymond, lived next door to us. Arthur and Dick were a lot older, and Raymond was enough older that we usually had different interests.

I probably played with the Elwood boys more than any of the others. Dexter Elwood was less than a year older. Everybody called him Bingy. His brother George was about a year younger. We called him JoJo. They had another brother, Robert, but he was quite a bit older and we didn't see him around very much.

In 1949, Mr. Elwood wanted to do some repair work on his floor furnace. There wasn't enough room in the crawl space for him to work comfortably, so he asked Bingy, JoJo, and me to dig a channel under the house from the crawl space opening to the furnace. We pretended that we were miners. We used hoes, shovels, a small pickax, and a wheelbarrow to remove quite a bit of dirt. There was a furnace vent in one of the bedrooms and Mrs. Elwood would pass snacks down to us. Celery sticks filled with peanut butter were the Elwood boys' favorite.

A week or two after Christmas, the children in the neighborhood would gather the old Christmas trees and take them to one of the vacant lots across the street. Mrs. Elwood and some of the other adults would supervise us as we made a huge bonfire.

We had a really great wagon. It was an Aero Flight wagon, built by Globe Biltwell. It had a shape something like a 1930s Chrysler Airflow. Ours was the only one I've ever seen with pneumatic tires, but the tires wouldn't hold air for very long. If we didn't use it for several days, the tires would go flat. Since it was really hard to use it that way, Robert or I would pull it up to the gas station on the corner of 109th and San Pedro to fill the tires with air. We could have two or three hours of fun with the wagon before the tires began to go flat again.

We sometimes played a variation on "blind man's bluff" on our front lawn. One of my friends had a pair of war surplus goggles with red lenses. If you wore them at dusk, it was almost like wearing a blindfold. All the kids would run around, taunting the person wearing the goggles, until a car drove by. The headlights of the car gave just enough illumination to allow the person who was "it" to see everyone, and the object was to hide before you got tagged.

At other times, especially if we had several kids in our backyard, we would put on skits. Three or four of us would be the actors, and the rest would be the audience. The audience would sit on our picnic table and benches, and the actors would go inside the woodshed to rehearse. It seems to me that half of the time the skit would involve some sort of monster like Frankenstein or a mummy. During the skit, the child playing the monster part would move toward the audience, moaning and making menacing gestures. Despite knowing what was coming, the kids in the audience would scream and try to run away. We definitely had overactive imaginations!

In the spring, when it became breezy, we would all fly kites. One of my friends had a contraption that he would place on the kite string. It was shaped like a miniature kite and had a parachute hanging below it. The wind would blow this contraption up the kite string until it got to the kite itself, and then the parachute was released. Several kids would run down the street, hoping the parachute would land in an open area, or in the yard of a nice neighbor and not a crabby neighbor.

In the summer, my parents would take us to the beach. Sometimes we would go to Belmont Shore, in Long Beach, but more often we went to Hermosa Beach. As they drove southwest from our house, the area became more open. Fewer and fewer houses and commercial buildings were visible. As we approached the beach, we crested a hilly area. From the top we could see the Pacific Ocean. I always exclaimed, "There's the ocean!" As many times as I saw it, it was as if I was seeing it for the first time.

One of my favorite indoor toys was an American Flyer electric train. I thought it looked better than the more popular Lionel electric trains. The American Flyer had two tracks while the Lionel ran on three tracks. The American Flyer trains were slightly smaller and were built to a more realistic scale. I also had a collection of British-made toy cars. Another of my favorites was a View Master. You could buy disks with stereoscopic pictures that slipped inside the View Master. We had a few disks with children's stories, but most of our disks were of national parks and other scenic places. I'm sure it helped cultivate my appreciation of the outdoors.

෴෴෴෴෴෴෴෴෴෴

My most vivid early memory was attending a birthday party for George Elwood. It was August 1945. We were in his backyard when Mrs. Elwood came out the back door. She was obviously excited. Waving her arms over her head, she shouted, "The war is over!" The Elwoods had a huge handbell that Mrs. Elwood used to call her children home. She gave the bell to George, passed out pots and pans and large spoons to the rest of us, and led us up and down the street, clanging and banging in celebration.

෴෴෴෴෴෴෴෴෴෴

I started kindergarten in September 1945. Like my brothers and sister before me, I attended what we called the 109th Street School. It was actually McKinley Avenue School, but I can't remember anybody calling it that. I drove by the old school recently and, in fact, it is now officially the 109th Street School. The school was an impressive two-story brick building with a slate roof. I can still remember the smell of cedar chips that the janitor spread on the hardwood floor as he swept. Today, the only part left of the original brick school is the auditorium.

The walk to school was not long. I'd walk about eight houses east on 109th Street, south through the alley toward 109th Place, then diagonally across a vacant lot toward Avalon. The crossing guard was at the corner of 109th Place and Avalon. From Avalon it was a very short block and a half to the school yard. It would have been closer to cross Avalon at 109th Street instead of 109th Place, but this was against the rules.

Kindergarten, like the other elementary grades, was divided into two semesters: A and B. I began in A, but for some reason I never went to the B part. When I finished A, I went straight to the first grade. This made me quite a bit younger than the other students. In the fourth grade I was kept back one semester so I more closely matched my classmates' age, but I was still the youngest person in my class.

I believe it was in the fourth grade that the teacher invited me to put on a puppet show for the class. Robert and I had a pair of matching hand puppets. Each puppet had a very flexible, rubber-like face and head, with a large beaky nose and protruding chin. As you slipped your hand inside, you would put your thumb and ring finger into the arms of the puppet, your first finger went into the nose, and your middle finger went into the chin. By manipulating your fingers, you could make the puppet's arms move and its mouth open and close. I think my show must have been pretty awful, but the other kids seemed to enjoy it.

I got "mugged" once on the way to school. I was in the fourth grade and was walking south through the alley. An older boy was walking rapidly in the other direction. He pushed me down and threw my lunch box against a nearby garage. He didn't hurt me and he left as quickly as he had come. My two main concerns were whether he had broken my thermos, and if I was going to be late for school. I had never been late before, and for some reason I had a real fear of this. I checked the thermos and it was OK, but when I got to the crossing guard she said, "You'd better hurry or you'll be late." This fed my anxiety. I got to my classroom as the teacher was checking the students to see if they had clean hands. For some reason tears started to fill my eyes. The teacher noticed and I quickly became the center of attention. This added to my distress. I reluctantly told her what had happened. I was taken to the principal's office and had to give a description of my "attacker" to the police. The school made a big fuss out of what was really a very minor incident.

The music education teacher at 109th Street School was Miss Evelyn Sharp. She also played the organ at the Inglewood Methodist Church. Our family attended this church during the 1940s. Some Sundays I would quietly slip into a cloakroom near the front of the sanctuary. From there I had a clear view of the organ. I watched in fascination as her hands traveled across the keyboard.

One thing that irked me while I was at 109th Street School was the fact that I was following my brother Robert. He was an exceptional student, and I was always being compared to him. It seemed to me that all the teachers knew him. I would be walking across the school playground and a teacher would notice me and say, "Aren't you Robert Daggett's little brother?" If I was running when I should have been walking, the teacher would add, "Your brother probably wouldn't do that!"

I never liked getting up in front of the class, at least not as myself. If I were part of a skit, or participating in some activity, it was fine. But if I was supposed to work at the blackboard or read something aloud I hated it. I usually knew the material, and I usually did fine, but it was something I really tried to avoid. When the teacher was scanning the class for someone to come forward, I tried to make myself as invisible as possible. I'd crouch down behind the student in front of me, hoping the teacher's gaze would go over my head.

Once, probably in the fourth grade, I was on the playground after lunch when I wanted to let my "girl friend" know that I liked her. The girl's name was Deanna Olson. I guess I'd seen too many Hollywood musicals. In the movies, it seemed to me that every time a man wanted to express something with emotion he would sing. Deanna had just gotten off the swings when I approached her singing, "Because of You." Tony Bennett made a recording of the song about this time and these were the only love song lyrics I knew. Deanna and most of the other nearby students looked at me like I was nuts. But she did say later that she liked me too.

Our family has always enjoyed camping. Before I was born, and when I was still an infant, my parents used a tent. My father felt that camping with four kids, and putting up a tent each night, was just too much trouble. During World War II, he scrounged some material and built a travel trailer. It was a simple box about four feet high when collapsed. When we got to our destination the top could be raised and the sides snapped into place. It was one of the first of this kind of convertible camping trailers. My father built in a Coleman stove and designed a drawer lined with galvanized sheet metal that we used as an icebox. If we stopped along the road to have lunch, I'd be sent into the trailer to get the milk out of the icebox. Since I was the smallest child, I could get around inside the collapsed trailer.

The first trip I remember well was in 1946. We went to Zion, Bryce, and Yellowstone National Parks. The night before we left home, my parents told me we were going to start very early in the morning, and they told me to sleep in my clothes. I thought this was neat. It added to my sense of adventure. My father woke me up about four in the morning and I was the first one in the car.

The next year, we went to Sequoia National Park. One of the sites to visit there, in addition to the gigantic redwood trees, is Moro Rock. The top of this granite monolith is 6,725 feet above sea level. There is a path, mostly very steep rock stairs, that leads to the top. Now they have railing, made of iron pipes, which helps keep the hikers from falling over the edge. But, in 1947, the "railing" consisted of a chain draped between widely spaced posts. There is no flat area on the top. It is like standing on the pointed end of an egg. In our photo album is a picture of the four Daggett kids standing on the top of Moro Rock. You can see that I'm not too comfortable. My seven-year-old fingers are wrapped around the chain in a death grip.

In 1948, my father rebuilt the trailer into a more conventional design. He used the same basic chassis, but he built permanent walls and covered them in aluminum. I remember helping him rivet the skin. I would go inside the trailer and hold a heavy piece of iron against the rivets as he set them in place.

We took many interesting trips in these first two trailers. In addition to our trips to most of the major national parks, we went all the way to North Carolina in 1952 to visit my mother's family. We made it a point to visit state capitols, and often toured museums and manufacturing facilities. I've toured lumber mills, bottling plants, smelters, auto assembly plants, and a host of other interesting places.

One of my favorite destinations was the eastern High Sierra. We camped beside Rock Creek, near Tom's Place, a number of times.

This is where I caught my first fish. In those days the campsites were under the pines, just a few feet from the creek. I spent hours exploring up and down the creek and hiking in the surrounding hills.

There was something special about going to sleep with the sound of the creek in the background, or sitting in the trailer during a summer afternoon rain shower. Raindrops would bounce off the trailer's aluminum roof, sometimes accompanied by bright flashes of lightning and the crack of thunder. When the rain stopped, I'd step out and take a deep breath. The air had a certain feeling, which is hard to describe. All of the mountain smells seemed to be intensified. Even now, on a warm summer evening, a sound or a smell will remind me of those times. If I close my eyes and concentrate, I can almost hear the water in the creek tumbling over the rocks and smell the mixture of pine trees and mountain sage. Some of my most cherished childhood memories are of the eastern High Sierra. It was a wonderful place for a young boy to experience nature.

Several times a year we would go on Sunday picnics. Not just to a neighborhood park, but on a two or three hour drive. We usually went with the Sperry family. My father and Mr. Sperry both worked for Western Electric. We had other things in common too. They were Methodists. They had four children. And they liked many of the same things we did: music, the outdoors, travel, etc. We often drove up to Charleton Flats in the Angeles National Forest. Other times we would drive to Idyllwild or Twentynine Palms, or up toward Palmdale to see the wildflowers. We would get up early on a Sunday morning, meet the Sperrys at a pre-determined location along the way, have breakfast at a coffee shop, and then drive for another hour or two until we got to our destination. We would play or explore the area until lunch was ready. After lunch the adults would visit as we kids played some more. We often played word games like Anagrams. In the late afternoon we would drive another two or three hours back home. This was long before there were any freeways, and I can remember driving for miles through orange groves, with eucalyptus trees lining both sides of the roads.

    ℘   *℘*   *℘*   *℘*   *℘*

The Lundys, our neighbors up the street, bought a television in 1947. It had a large cabinet about two feet wide and three or four feet high, but the picture tube was only seven inches in diameter. This was the common size that year. Most of the kids in the neighborhood would gather at the Lundy house in the afternoon. We would watch in fascination as the black and white test pattern appeared. Television programming didn't usually start until late afternoon, but even watching the test pattern was a novelty.

We got our first television in 1948. My parents didn't go to a store to purchase it. My father built it himself! I remember all the resistors, condensers (capacitors), transformers, and tubes spread out on the dining room table. It had a twelve-inch picture tube and seemed really large compared to the Lundy's seven-inch screen. It could also receive FM radio.

In these early television days, I watched very few regularly scheduled programs. I watched a puppet show called *Time for Beany*, a science fiction series called *Space Patrol*, and some westerns like *Hopalong Cassidy*. When people talk about the early years of television, they often mention Milton Berle and Sid Caesar, but I don't remember watching them more than a few times. Milton Berle, especially, seemed way overblown to me. I think my viewing habits were considered odd by some of my peers. I enjoyed programs like *Omnibus*, a semi-cultural potpourri. I also enjoyed *The Bell Telephone Hour* and *The Voice of Firestone*.

One program that none of my friends would have been caught dead watching was called *The Last Word*, moderated by Bergan Evans, a professor of literature at Northwestern University. A panel of experts would answer viewers' questions about sentence structure, grammar, and correct usage. The questions were answered with humor, and I found it interesting. I remember at the end of one program Bergan Evans expounded on what he called, "the Evans Law of Greed and Gratitude." He said that if someone was given all the money in the world, except for ten dollars, and these ten dollars were given to another person, the person who got the larger amount would probably say, "What did *that* person do to get ten dollars?"

❧   ❧   ❧   ❧   ❧

My father was always puttering around at the workbench or building something. It seemed he could build anything. He built our first house, our first two travel trailers, our first television, and dozens of other items that enriched my life.

I think I got my inclination to build things from him. Of the four children, I think I'm the only one who enjoyed sawing and nailing and working with electrical things. When I was eleven I built what I called, "my invention." It was a wooden panel, about three feet wide, with a variety of electrical switches, lights, and buzzers. I wired this together using parts that my father had salvaged from some of the telephone offices he had supervised.

Like my father, I've also completed several major electronics projects. In the late 1950s, we worked together to build our first stereo music system. I assembled most of the parts while he did the soldering. I designed the base reflex speaker cabinets and he did the finish carpentry. We built another stereo system in the early 1970s, and over the years I've built several pieces of electronic test equipment. I also built a high voltage Tesla coil from old television parts. It looked like something out of a mad scientist movie, with bright electric sparks arcing back and forth as they traveled up between two vertical rods.

Growing Up

In 1949, my parents bought a lot in Downey, California, right in the middle of an orange grove. Our street was named Wiley-Burke Avenue. At that time Wiley-Burke was just one block long, ending at the edge of another orange grove to our north.

My parents designed our house, and we took many trips back and forth from 109th Street to watch the progress as it was built. We had a big front yard and wide areas on each side of the house. My father planted the lawn in a low ground cover called dichondra, which was very fashionable in the 1950s. It made a beautiful lawn but required a lot of attention.

The living room was at the back of the house, with large windows looking out to the covered patio and backyard. We removed quite a number of orange trees on the lot to make room for the house, but we still had eight trees left. The smell of the orange blossoms was wonderful. We moved into our new house the day after Christmas in 1950.

The families on our block were mostly upper middle class. Most of the fathers had management positions in large corporations or owned their own small businesses. Most of the mothers were stay-at-home moms, involved in church and civic organizations.

I was in the middle of the fifth grade when we moved. The closest elementary school was Gallatin School, a little over a mile from our new home. It seemed quite a long distance compared to the walk to 109th Street School, which had been only two short blocks. At the end of my first day at Gallatin, I got on the wrong school bus to come home. I had never taken a school bus before and realized something wasn't right when I was the last one left on the bus. The driver asked me where I lived and brought me to my stop. About half the time I walked to school. I would walk east on Lubec Street, or through the orange grove to Paramount Boulevard. Then I'd work my way north to Gallatin Road and east to the school. On the way home, I'd sometimes go south from the school to Florence Avenue, then west on Florence to Wiley-Burke.

The school was built in a modified California Mission style. It was U-shaped, with a red tile roof, and all the rooms opened onto a covered portico. It was rather small, with just five or six classrooms. Downey was growing rapidly in the early 1950s, and shortly after I arrived at Gallatin School they started building additional classrooms. These were in the more conventional California school bungalow design. I spent my sixth grade year in one of these new schoolrooms. As I look back, I think the sixth grade was the first year I could truthfully say I enjoyed school. I had many happy times at the 109th Street School, and I was a pretty good student, but there were times when I felt intimidated by the teachers.

My sixth grade teacher was Mrs. Truxaw. I think all of the students liked her. Her husband worked for a newspaper, and she taught us the importance of writing clearly and to the point. She told the class that when we read anything, we should consider who wrote it, who the intended reader was, and what point the author was trying to make. She wanted us to read with a critical eye. She also encouraged us in science and art. I feel fortunate that my early education took place in this atmosphere. At 109th Street School we had regular weekly visits by a music education teacher. At Gallatin we had exposure to art and the sciences. I also had the opportunity to take several interesting school-sponsored field trips.

The sixth grade graduation ceremony at Gallatin included an opportunity for each student to ring the mammoth school bell. This large bell was originally on the roof of the building, but, because of seismic concerns, it had been relocated to a cement pad on the ground in front of the school. The graduating students lined up and came forward to ring the bell as our names were called.

I started junior high in September 1952. There was no junior high school in the north part of Downey, so I attended Downey High School for one semester. North Junior High (now called Griffiths Middle School) was completed the following January, almost literally in our backyard. This was fortunate, because I had started playing the saxophone the previous year and I needed to carry it back and forth to school.

I had taken piano lessons when I was eight years old, but I guess I was too young to appreciate them. And I had trouble making my hands work independently. I could play a melody with my right hand or chords with my left. I just had trouble doing them both at the same time. I think I was an exasperation to my teacher, Mrs. Blythe. If I made a mistake, I'd go back to the beginning. She'd tell me, "Just go on. You don't have to start the whole thing over again."

The saxophone was different. I really enjoyed it. The first two pieces I learned were the "Washington Post March" and "Abide With Me." I wasn't a virtuoso but I was good enough to play in the school band.

Mr. Stillman, the Downey High School band director, was my first saxophone teacher. During the summer months, my mother would drop me off at Downey High for my lessons and give me money for bus fare to get home. The two-mile walk home would have been easy without carrying my saxophone, but at eleven years old, it was a task carrying it that far. Even so, I sometimes pocketed the bus fare and walked.

When North Junior High opened, I took private lessons from Mr. Norvell, the band director there. He was a nice man, but he had a habit of borrowing my saxophone to demonstrate some technique he wanted me to try. When he gave the saxophone back, his saliva was still hanging from the reed. Yuch!

I remember one of the things he would say was, "Richard, don't toot." He wanted a smoother transition between notes. A friend of mine found an old wire recording labeled "Norvelle/private students." On it were several segments of different instruments playing music and scales. It including a saxophonist doing fancy scales and, as far as I know, I was his only private saxophone student, so it might have been a recording of me. I don't remember Mr. Norvell making a recording. At least he never mentioned it. If he did, it was probably to review his student's progress.

I also sang in the mixed glee club. My voice hadn't changed yet, so I usually sang in the alto section. I was told I had a good voice, and singing was something that really gave me pleasure. As I remember, we sang a lot of Stephen Foster songs. At several school assemblies I would switch between playing the saxophone and singing. I would begin on stage with the band and, at an appropriate time, I would slip out the side curtains and take my place on the risers with the other singers.

Before Wiley-Burke Avenue was extended, we would play in the orange grove north of our house. We built bicycle paths between the rows of trees, and made a ramp at the end of our street out of mounded dirt. We would pedal our bicycles as fast as we could down the street and up the ramp, seeing who could jump the farthest. On one occasion, the front wheel came off a friend's bicycle as he was in midair. When he landed, the empty front fork dug into the soft ground and he flew over the handlebars, hitting an orange tree. He lay motionless for what seemed like ages, and we were sure he had broken his neck. Thankfully, he just had the wind knocked out of him.

Sometimes we would play "war," throwing overripe oranges as hand grenades. We often congregated in the west end of the grove, near the Rio Hondo River. The usually dry river would sometimes overflow its banks during winter rain storms, and it had created a wide, flat, sandy area that was ideal for our activities. We would often see jackrabbits running between the high bushes and bamboo that edged the river, so we named the area "Rabbit Town."

One or two blocks from our house, in any direction, brought me into farm life. It was just one block south, across Florence Avenue, to a huge bean field. A block west of our house was a seven-acre field where a man grew flowers for the wholesale florist industry. Two blocks west was the Rio Hondo Dairy. Less than fifty yards north of us was the orange grove.

Most of these agricultural areas were quietly disappearing, and in 1952 they took the orange grove out to build houses. We kids were sorry to see the grove gone, but we found ways to make the new construction site our own private playground.

𝒢 𝒢 𝒢 𝒢 𝒢

I was never passionate about team sports. Baseball was not very interesting to me, and I never had a bat or glove of my own. I was pretty good in the few flag football and soccer games we had at school, but it wasn't something I thought about often. We had a basketball hoop mounted above our garage door, and even this was just a way to pass some time with friends. I did, however, enjoy track and field events. I was a very good runner, and could hurdle and long jump very well for my age. Many of the boys in my class would moan when the coach would tell us to take laps around the field. Not me. I sometimes ran facing backward as a friendly taunt to my classmates who seemed to be winded after less than half a lap. I also enjoyed badminton and croquet and, when I was twelve, I built a pair of stilts that raised me about eighteen inches off the ground. I was quite good, if I do say so myself. I could even go up and down stairs.

However, my favorite outdoor activities were roller skating, bicycling, and golf. I enjoyed hitting golf balls from our front lawn into the orange grove. I sometimes spent hours hitting balls and retrieving them. I had to make adjustments because my father's clubs were right-handed and I was left-handed. I would hear some of my father's friends talk about fading the ball or drawing it around some obstacle. I wasn't sure what they meant. I always hit the ball perfectly straight, right where I was aiming. I thought that was the way you were supposed to hit it. My brother Robert and I sometimes made miniature golf courses out of bricks placed in patterns across the lawn or any available bare dirt.

𝒢 𝒢 𝒢 𝒢 𝒢

Saturday afternoon barbecues were a tradition at our house. My father made his own special hamburger press, and weighed the meat with a postal scale so each patty was uniform. My mother bought roasts and had the butcher grind the meat. She wanted to see the meat before it was turned into hamburger. We always had an abundance of patties in the freezer, because we weren't sure how many would join us. Everyone knew it was barbecue time at the Daggetts' place, and most Saturdays we had friends and relatives who "just stopped by to say hello." Of course, my mother always insisted they stay and eat.

During the fall and winter of 1952–53, several friends and I decided to take ballroom dancing lessons. I don't remember whose idea it was. We went to dance school in Huntington Park and learned the waltz and fox trot, as well as social etiquette. I doubt that many kids would do this today, but at the time it was a pleasant diversion. J.D. Williams, Bob Rechin, Karla and Jerry Watkins, and I would dress up in our best clothes and polish our manners. It was fun, and put me more at ease the few times we had school dances, although nobody ever danced the waltz or fox trot. Downey in the 1950s was a great place to be a kid.

~~ ~~ ~~ ~~ ~~

I turned thirteen on June 14, 1953, and a few days later graduated from the seventh grade. At the end of June we went camping at Rock Creek. We camped near where a retired minister and his wife were camped, and one afternoon they offered to take Robert and me fishing. We drove to a spot on Rock Creek below Tom's Place. The couple pointed out a location on the creek that they thought looked promising. The water tumbled over the rocks on the far side of the creek, but there was a quiet pool on my side. I dropped my line in the water and waited.

To my surprise I caught a good size trout in less than five minutes. The spot I was fishing wasn't very big and I figured I caught the only fish there. I tried other spots up and down the creek with no success. When I returned to the original location about two hours later, the minister's wife was still fishing in the same quiet pool. She had four more fish. I felt sort of foolish.

I didn't have a creel to carry my single fish, so the minister showed me how to cut a large forked twig and thread it through the fish's gills. I hung my fish from this and walked back to camp. I probably looked like a character from *Huckleberry Finn,* but I felt like a mighty hunter bringing home my prize.

Taking a Detour

We got home from Rock Creek in time to sign up for my second session of swimming lessons at Downey High School. At least that was the plan. Of course, things don't always work out as planned. The first indication I had that something was wrong was waking Friday morning, July 17, 1953, with a stiff neck and back. It was not only stiff, but it really hurt too. Putting my clothes on was very, very uncomfortable.

I had a couple of severe headaches the day before, but they both went away after an hour or so. I don't remember ever having a headache as a child and, in any case, I wasn't going to let these headaches spoil my summer fun. I ran down the street and, with every stride, my brain felt like it wanted to leave my skull. It hurt, but I wasn't concerned. I'd occasionally hear friends and family members complain of headaches, and they always seemed to feel better later.

This back pain was different. I'd never known anything like this. I stayed in bed until mid-morning, when my mother called my father at work. He came home and they took me to see Dr. Hershey at the Ross-Loos Clinic in Huntington Park. The doctor did some tests, mostly to do with my reflexes. He said I should be taken to the Los Angeles County General Hospital.

We arrived at County General and entered the Communicable Disease Ward. The ward was housed in a very old, red brick building on Zonal Avenue, just west of the main hospital building. Everything inside seemed old too. I was put in a bed and they began giving me more tests. Every time a doctor came by he would ask me to try sitting up in bed without using my arms. This seemed to have some special significance. I did this about a dozen times and had no difficulty.

In the afternoon they did a spinal tap. They told me it was a test to see if I had polio. Everyone in the early 1950s had seen March of Dimes posters with iron lungs and kids with leg braces and crutches, but polio was not something I thought about much as a child. I didn't think any more about polio than I did about getting hit by a truck. I don't remember my parents making much of a fuss over it either.

The tap itself was very painful, but what hurt even more was trying to get in the knees-to-chin position that a tap required. They kept asking me to bend forward more, but the pain in my back was really intense.

I spent the rest of the afternoon in a small alcove off a much larger room. I could see other children in the larger room. Although they were all in bed, they didn't seem to be very sick. Some of them appeared to be playing games of some kind.

That night my legs began to ache and, shortly after midnight, I started to have trouble sitting up. I needed to urinate and I could see a urinal on the nightstand next to my bed. I tried to reach for it but my arms wouldn't cooperate. With great effort I finally reached it, but I was completely exhausted.

I didn't know how a person was supposed to feel if they had polio, but not being able to sit up told me I had it. I distinctly remember saying to myself, "Uh-oh, I think I have it." When my parents came to visit on Saturday I told them the same thing, "I think I have it." I said it almost apologetically. I knew my parents didn't want to hear this.

Sometime late Saturday afternoon they wheeled me into a small room where they started an IV. Then some people in surgical gowns wheeled me to another room that looked like a dentist's office. Here they performed a tracheotomy.

A tracheotomy—without an "s"—is the name of the surgical procedure to open an airway in your trachea, or "windpipe." A tracheostomy—with an "s"—is the incision left after the operation. I now have a tracheostomy, pronounced with a long "a." Those of us familiar with tracheostomies usually refer to them as "trachs," still pronounced with a long "a."

The operation was performed with a local anesthetic. I was wide awake, and I could watch the doctors bending over me as they worked. The one who seemed to be the leader wore goggles over his glasses because, he said, "It keeps the patient's breath from fogging them up." There must have been several people present who were unfamiliar with the operation, because the doctor with the goggles gave a running commentary. Everybody in the room obviously knew what they were doing to me. Everybody in the room but me!

Up until this time I had moments of apprehension, but I was never really frightened. Of course, I wondered what was happening, but, except for the spinal tap, nothing that had been done was very painful and everybody acted like things were going fine. Then the doctor doing the tracheotomy made one final cut and air started sucking in and out of the hole he made in my windpipe. I thought he must have done something wrong. I tried to ask them what had happened, but every time I tried to talk, more air bubbled up out of the hole. Now I really was frightened.

When they finished the operation, they put me in a tank respirator, more commonly known as an iron lung. As my head was sliding through the opening, I vomited. I tried to apologize, but the words wouldn't come out. And blood seemed to be all over the place. *My blood!*

I either passed out or they gave me a shot of something to make me sleep, because the next thing I remember was waking up in a large room. There was a mirror over my head and, in the mirror, I could see a row of large black bellows across the room. They were going up and down. I didn't know much about respirators, but I figured one of them must be making me breathe. I tried to figure which one it was by timing my breathing with the motion of each bellows. None of them seemed to match my breathing pattern. It wasn't until later in the day, when my mirror was adjusted upward, that I realized those bellows were all attached to the underside of other respirators. I couldn't see mine because it was beneath me.

I was in a Drinker-Collins "iron lung." The Drinker machines were bluish green and had the bellows on the bottom of the respirator.

These were the most common type of tank respirator in Los Angeles County. The Emerson "iron lung" was a pale yellow, almost sickly, color and had the bellows on the end. The Emerson machines were less sophisticated and cheaper to manufacture. They were more common in other parts of the country. Both types made a low whooshing sound as they worked to keep us breathing.

An iron lung helps a person breathe by creating a rhythmic negative pressure within the tank. This negative pressure creates a partial vacuum and the patient's chest wall expands trying to fill this vacuum. When the chest expands the patient draws in air, mimicking natural breathing. The pressure and rate can vary for each patient. Those of us with significant paralysis of our breathing muscles often had additional air forced into our lungs through a tracheostomy. The tracheostomy can also be used to suction mucous from our lungs. I'm sure the tracheostomy saved my life.

After a few days, I got used to the routine: two shots in the morning, one at noon, one at night, bath every day, and an enema every other day. Yuch! I had blood taken for tests every third day, usually out of my leg or groin. Ouch! Some people might think that if a person can't move, then they can't feel either. Let me clear that up right now. Polio does not affect your senses. You are able to feel everything. If something looks like it would be painful, it probably *is* painful!

I couldn't swallow, so they inserted a tube through my nose and down into my stomach to feed me, and I still had the intravenous tube in my arm. Later they moved the IV to my leg. When they did this, they performed what they called a "cut down," similar to what is now called a central line. They cut open a vein in my ankle and inserted the IV tube directly into the vein. That was one of the things that really hurt, both when it was opened and again when it was closed. I assume they must have used some local anesthetic, but it sure didn't feel like it.

My mother drove to the hospital to visit almost every afternoon and both of my parents came in the evening. I'm sure it was a difficult time for them. I was their youngest child, and I was very, very ill with bulbospinal polio, the most severe form of this disease. I learned later that, in addition to polio, I had a life-threatening case of pneumonia.

It was probably more difficult for the parents than for the young patients. Imagine entering a room filled with these huge metal tanks making their whooshing sound. All you can see are heads sticking out one end of each tank, and you know that one of these heads belongs to your child.

I've heard from many polio survivors who felt isolated from their families while in the hospital. They state that their parents were not allowed to visit them for several weeks. Even when they could visit, they would be kept separated, either behind a glass partition or outside the building completely, only able to wave to their child through a window. Many patients were visited only on Sundays or some other rare occasion. This was not the case at Los Angeles County General Hospital. As I relate above, my parents were allowed to visit me twice a day, with restrictions on actual physical contact. When I was transferred to Rancho Los Amigos, we had regular visiting hours. These were Saturday and Sunday afternoons and evenings, and Wednesday evenings. Parents could visit their children on any day and at any reasonable time. Perhaps the doctors and hospital administrators in Los Angeles County had a more enlightened perspective than those in other parts of the country.

My father began a daily journal of the events surrounding my illness and hospitalization. He never mentioned it, and I didn't know about it until after his death, when I was going through his papers. I believe this journal was his way of coping with the strain and sadness he and my mother must have endured.

Here are some excerpts from the first few entries:

Friday, July 17: Dr. Hershey examined him and gave us an order to take him to the CD building at the General Hospital. Arrived about 11:30 a.m. They asked us a lot of questions and gave Richard an examination. He said he felt "Pretty good." The doctor told us he had no muscular weakness at that time.

Saturday, July 18: Arrived at the hospital at 2:00 p.m. Richard was suffering some discomfort and said, "I have it", meaning polio.

He showed us the difficulty he had moving his arms. We returned home somewhat apprehensive. At 9:00 p.m. Dr. Miller called and said Richard developed some difficulty breathing and they were planning to put him in an Iron Lung later in the evening. He called again about 11:30 and suggested we come there. We went immediately. We couldn't see the doctor until 2:15 a.m. He explained they put Richard in the Lung as a precaution and to save his strength. We went home feeling pretty low.

Sunday, July 19: Called the hospital at 9:00 a.m. The nurse said Richard had a quiet night and that we could see him. We went right over and visited with him for 10 minutes. He seemed in good spirits, under the circumstances, and was comfortable. Talked to one of the Drs. and he explained some things about polio to us. As long as the patient has a fever it is still "working". After that they can determine the extent of nerve damage. There is nothing to do but wait for two or three days for the answer. They will be anxious days for us. Went to the hospital again in the evening. Richard is a very sick boy.

Monday, July 20: I left work at noon. Went home for lunch and we went to the hospital. The nurse was working on Richard when we saw him. The Dr. said he had developed pneumonia. Still a very sick boy. We returned to the hospital at 7:00 p.m. We were rewarded with the first hopeful sign. Richard seemed in good spirits and the nurse said his temperature was down a little. We came home clinging to that slim thread of hope.

Tuesday, July 21: Came home for lunch and went to the hospital. The nurse was working on Richard so we had to wait in the hall a few minutes before we could see him. He is very sick but the Dr. said his fever is slightly lower. He also told us that Richard has a better than even chance to pull through. Returned to the hospital at 7:00 p.m. Richard was asleep when we went in but the nurse awakened him. He seemed glad to see us. I asked him if he was discouraged and he shook his head to indicate a definite "NO!" That spirit can't lose and I'm real sure he will win.

I treasure this journal. It is important historically, but even more important to me is the written record of my parents' thoughts and concerns.

Everyone had to wear gowns and a few people wore masks when they were on the patient units in the Communicable Disease Ward. Men, who I assumed were doctors, would often stop by my respirator. They would talk *about* me, but never *to* me. It was almost as if I were a bug in a petri dish. This heightened my sense of apprehension. Were they preparing to do some different tests? Would they be painful?

The nights were the worst times. They kept some of the lights on and there was always someone who needed attention. I didn't want to sleep anyway because, when I did sleep, a little bit of the air being forced into my lungs by the respirator would leak out my nostrils. When I awoke, aerated mucous covered part of my face. This was very disturbing to me. Try to imagine lying on your back, while you have the worst cold you can envision. Now imagine that while you are sleeping you are continuously and unconsciously blowing your nose. And you are blowing your nose without even using a tissue. Yuch! I don't remember other patients mentioning this but I'm guessing there must have been others with this problem. It was caused by the almost complete paralysis of my breathing and swallowing muscles. Any slight control I had while awake disappeared when I slept. I had this problem for almost two weeks.

I was very naïve. I had no real understanding of how serious my condition was. Oh, I knew that I was completely paralyzed, but the long-term impact did not sink in. My greatest concern was that I might miss the first day of school. Part of this may have been because my only direct knowledge of polio was through the Elwood boys. They both had polio in 1948. They were in the hospital for about three weeks, and then reappeared without any visible aftereffects.

As I lay motionless and on life support, I thought about starting school in September. After a couple of weeks, I realized I wasn't going to suddenly jump up and start walking, but I still thought I'd leave the hospital before school began. I could visualize going back to school on crutches or maybe with a slight limp. In a kind of demented way this appealed to me. I figured all the girls would fawn over me.

Perhaps a person's mind tries to protect itself from reality. Or perhaps my mind was just overly dense. Before polio I bit my fingernails. I tried to break the habit but not very successfully. In the iron lung I couldn't bring my fingers to my mouth. After a few days I could tell my nails were longer. I mentioned this to my parents, and my father said he'd buy me a nail clipper and file if I continued to let them grow.

Here I was, encased in a large, 800-pound metal cylinder with just my head sticking out. I couldn't move, breathe, or swallow. But when my father offered to buy me my own personal nail clipper, I felt as if I'd just won the lottery.

᪣᪣   ᪣᪣   ᪣᪣   ᪣᪣   ᪣᪣

I don't recollect exactly when I found out that I would be transferred to Rancho Los Amigos Hospital (now Rancho Los Amigos National Rehabilitation Center). My first thought was, "No way!" We had driven by Rancho several times when our house in Downey was being built. It had always been described to me as the "old folks' home." There was no way I was going to an old folks' home. Rancho had been the county poor farm from the late 1800s through the 1930s. I didn't realize that Rancho had been gradually changing. It had become the largest of the thirteen respiratory centers funded by the National Foundation for Infantile Paralysis (March of Dimes).

Three weeks after I entered the Communicable Disease Ward at County General I was put in a huge ambulance built especially for tank respirators. A team of electricians followed as I was pushed through the corridors of the hospital and out to the ambulance loading ramp. They would alternately disconnect and reconnect my respirator to long electrical extension cords. My regular mirror was replaced by an unbreakable one made of polished metal, and the rear doors of the ambulance were left open so I could see out the back. This was in the closing months of the Korean conflict and we happened to enter the freeway in the middle of a military convoy. I could see a long line of Jeeps and transports following the ambulance. They stayed with us for a mile or two until our driver hit the siren and we pulled away, screaming down the freeway off ramp.

I was taken to Building 60 at Rancho. This was just an old, two-story stucco structure about sixty feet by one hundred and fifty feet, divided into four large rooms on the ground floor. There appeared to be eight to twelve patients in each room. There were several identical buildings in a row: Buildings 30, 40, 50, 60, and 70. My room in

34

Building 60 had all boys, from about eight to fourteen years old. The staff greeted me warmly and always had a positive attitude, at least around the patients. The whole atmosphere was that patients were going to get better. And most did.

While at County General, the only visitors I was allowed were my parents. At Rancho they allowed visits by other family members and friends. The Elwood boys and many of my school friends came by, but I think some of my friends were kept away by their parents. Polio is not contagious after three weeks, but some parents probably thought it was better to be safe than sorry.

After two weeks at Rancho, I was assigned a physical therapist. Her name was Miss Coler, known "affectionately" as "Killer Coler." Her first task was to stretch any of my muscles that had tightened from disuse. The only parts of my body that I could move by that time were the toes on my right foot. There was a lot of stretching to do! I was still unable to breathe on my own, so when my respirator was opened for therapy, I was hooked to positive air pressure directly into my tracheostomy.

Every day, prior to therapy, I would get hot packs. These were wool blankets that were steam heated and spun dry, then wrapped around my arms, legs, and body. They were very hot, and I got burned once. But that happened only once, and this was just carelessness by an inexperienced nurse. After a half hour, the hot packs began to get cold and clammy. The cold, damp wool made me itch, so it really felt good to have them removed and have the sweat toweled off. Some polio survivors talk about the awful smell of the hot packs, sort of like a wet, dirty dog. I agree that they did smell, but I didn't find it particularly objectionable. I actually enjoyed the moist heat.

About the same time I started therapy, they also began feeding me soft foods by mouth. It wasn't long before the tube was removed from my nose and I began eating regular meals. We often had soft-boiled eggs for breakfast. Sometimes they were nearly raw and, at other times, they were were as hard as golf balls. It didn't make any difference to the nursing attendants who fed me. As they cracked open the eggs, they would always say the eggs were "just right." It got to be an ongoing joke.

Sometimes my mother would prepare Lipton's chicken noodle soup and bring some to me in a thermos. The noodles were small enough to drink through a straw. There was a trick to eating because I had to time my swallowing with the respirator. An iron lung pretty much takes over your life. It is much stronger than a patient's weak muscles. It tells you when to breathe and how deeply to breathe.

Talking while in the respirator was very frustrating too. I would get in the middle of a word and have to stop and wait for the next breath. People using respirators often talk in sentence fragments.

This might be a good time to explain terminology. I use "tank" and "iron lung" interchangeably in my story when I refer to these large respirators. I think most people in the 1950s would probably be more familiar with the term iron lung, but, in the hospital, this type of respirator was usually referred to as a tank.

I quickly learned the emergency "code" of respiratory dependent patients. If our respirators malfunctioned, a tube became disconnected, or something happened that needed immediate attention, we were told to make a clicking sound with our tongue. This always brought a rapid response from the nurses.

＿＿＿＿ ＿＿＿＿ ＿＿＿＿ ＿＿＿＿ ＿＿＿＿

Once a week the hospital tested the back-up electric generator. With so many respirator dependent patients, it was vital that the hospital have a reliable source of emergency electricity. At noon, on the dot, the tank respirators and other equipment would go silent as the outside electricity was shut off. In a few seconds we'd hear the huge diesel engine start up. After a few more seconds, the engine was up to full speed and the transfer switch was thrown to the emergency generator. Everything would run on back-up power for about half an hour before they would switch back.

It was also vital that all employees know how to manually pump the tank respirators, just in case something catastrophic happened. Doctors, nurses, therapists, maintenance staff, and custodians had to learn. This was hard, physical work, but everyone was trained in this important exercise.

_6℮ᴝ   6℮ᴝ   6℮ᴝ   6℮ᴝ   6℮ᴝ_

Like many of the other patients in an iron lung, I had several personal items hanging near my head at the front of the tank. I had a small plastic dog that the Elwood boys had brought me, a photo of my brother Rodney in his Army uniform, a photo of one of my girl friends, and a photo of me throwing a football. The football photo was the last picture taken of me before polio. Looking back, I think having it on my respirator might have been my subconscious way of saying, "This is the _real_ me. Not the weak, emaciated kid you see with his head sticking out of this tank."

The mirror over my head was adjustable. On the back there was a wire frame that could hold books or magazines. Someone would have to come by periodically to turn the pages. Reading was a very slow process, but I kept up with my school work and read several books this way.

_6℮ᴝ   6℮ᴝ   6℮ᴝ   6℮ᴝ   6℮ᴝ_

I was almost completely paralyzed, but in most other respects I was a normal thirteen-year-old adolescent. It was while I was in the tank that I had my first wet dream. I still remember the dream that accompanied the event. I remember it as clearly as if it were yesterday. The dream had very little to do with sex, at least not as we would normally use that word. In the middle of the dream I woke up. At first I thought I was wetting the bed. A moment or two later I knew I wasn't wetting the bed, but I wasn't sure what was happening. After a while I figured it out.

I waited, frightened and embarrassed, for the first nurse to come by in the morning. She asked something like, "What's all this wet stuff?" or maybe, "What's all this white stuff?" I was too flustered to think straight, but I lied and told her I had no idea. It was never mentioned again. I had nocturnal emissions periodically while I was a patient at Rancho. It was always embarrassing to me, but nobody ever said a word about them.

In the early 1950s, thirteen-year-old boys didn't know much about their bodies, and even less about sex. I think I always knew that babies came from their mother. The stork story was just that—a story. From about eight years old I knew about intercourse. I saw a couple "doing it" one day while I was on the way to school. It wasn't something we talked about often and, I regret to say, like most of my peers I always called it by the "f" word. I was probably eleven before I found out about the connection between intercourse and babies. Boys at school talked about sex, but most of them knew as little as I did. Nobody used correct anatomical or physiological terms. Most of the boys seemed to have a fixation with large breasts, but that was never a turn-on for me.

Early in September we started the battle of the casts. It began with foot casts. Dr. McConaghal, along with Nino, from the plaster room, put casts on both of my feet. They came back in a few days, removed a crescent-shaped piece from the front of the cast, pushed the sole of my foot upward, and plastered it up again. This was to stretch my Achilles tendon and calf muscles. The trouble was, it also put pressure on my toes. The casts extended beyond the ends of my toes and, although I complained of soreness, everything looked fine. Nino came by a couple of times, but said he couldn't do anything without the doctor's approval. He tried to relieve the pressure by bending the casts away from my toes. I finally convinced Nino, and he convinced the doctor, that something wasn't right. When they cut the casts off, they could see that the skin on the side of my little toe had broken open. Blood oozed out, turning the cast red.

Most of the time things were pretty monotonous, although we did have movies once a week to break the routine. These were usually short films, but occasionally we had a full-length feature. A man would bring a 16-millimeter movie projector to the ward and place the large projection screen at one end of the room. Sometimes the beds and tank respirators would have to be moved around so that we could all see. One afternoon, they wheeled a group of us to Rancho's large auditorium to see a fully-staged production of Humperdink's opera, *Hansel and Gretel*, complete with orchestra and professional singers in costume. Other times we would be visited by some well-known personality. The first one I saw, after being at Rancho about a week, was Barbara Stanwyck.

Some strength was returning, especially to my legs, and I slowly regained some breathing tolerance: ten minutes, three times a day, then fifteen minutes, then twenty, etc. When I could breathe about one hour on my own, I graduated from the tank respirator to a chest respirator. This type of respirator covers just a person's torso, and works on the same principal as the larger tank respirator. It looked a little like a turtle's shell. It allowed me to lie on a bed, escaping the confines of the tank.

By Christmas 1953, I had enough breathing tolerance to visit home on a four-hour pass. Most of the patients were not afforded this luxury, because they lived too far from the hospital. But it was just two miles from Rancho to our house. A few days prior to my first visit home, my mother and father had to take lessons in how to operate the various pieces of equipment I had to take home with me: portable respirator, suction machine, etc.

The first time I went home I noticed something different, but I couldn't figure it out right away. Then it dawned on me. It was quiet. There were sounds at home, of course, but at Rancho there was a constant background noise of respirators and other equipment. It wasn't loud enough to bother anybody, but it was always present. The silence at home was kind of eerie until I got used it.

In January, I was transferred from Building 60 to Building 40 and my activities were stepped up. One of the first items on the list was to plug my trach tube with a temporary plug made of rolled up adhesive tape. It took several days for me to get used to breathing through my nose and mouth again, but then I could talk without putting my finger over the open trach tube.

The next thing they wanted me to try was standing, using a "standing board." This was a narrow wooden table with a gear arrangement so that a person strapped on it could be raised from a horizontal to a vertical position. I was told that before I could be allowed to stand, I needed a plaster "body jacket" to help support my back. They took me to the plaster room where I was suspended in a kind of rack made out of pipes. My head was in a harness, a sling supported each arm, and two slings supported each leg. More harnesses were added to each ankle and traction was applied. This allowed the doctors and Nino, the "cast man," free access to the main part of my body so that the plaster cast could be applied. The apparatus looked like a medieval torture machine, but there was actually very little discomfort. I did, however, have a feeling of extreme vulnerability from hanging suspended in midair. I felt really naked too. They put a stockinet over my torso that became the lining for the cast, but I was lucky if they left the stockinet long enough to cover my private parts. If the stockinet wasn't long enough, they sometimes placed a washcloth or small towel between my legs. I still felt naked.

With the plaster body jacket, I was allowed to sit on the side of the bed for a few minutes. I was even allowed to stand briefly and to sit in a wheelchair. Not for an extended period, but long enough for my parents to wheel me outside and look around.

Standing was a big milestone. I was very unsteady, but I could support my own weight without braces or crutches. This gave me hope that I would walk at some point.

By February 1954, I had improved enough so that I could breathe without any equipment for several hours a day. We were all looking forward to the move to the new facilities on the north side of Imperial Highway, but shortly before the big day came, I caught a cold and my left lung collapsed. It didn't actually collapse, that was just the term they used. The correct medical term is atelectasis. It was just before visiting hours on Sunday and, all of a sudden, I couldn't breathe. Pandemonium struck as I made the emergency clicking sound with my tongue! Nurses and attendants ran everywhere. I was lying on my bed, so they opened an unused tank respirator across the room, picked me up, and shoved me in. A curtain was pulled around the area, and in several minutes two doctors appeared with a portable x-ray machine. I was put on medication and remained in the tank for about three weeks.

I was still in the tank when we made the move to the north side of the highway. The move was very well coordinated. They moved more than 125 patients, many in iron lungs, in just four hours. My home for the next six weeks was Ward 502. The new 500 Building looked more like a country club than a hospital. The architecture of the main entrance had a very modern appearance, with a gently sloping roof and expansive floor-to-ceiling windows. The circular driveway in front of the main entrance was landscaped with tall palm trees and tropical plants.

The 500 Building had three patient wings: Wards 501, 502, and 503. Each ward had eight rooms, and each room was designed for eight patients. There was space for one hundred ninety-two patients. Most of the patients had some degree of respirator dependence. That was Rancho's specialty. The 500 Building also had outpatient clinics, several therapy rooms, and an indoor exercise pool.

After I got over my cold, I was allowed back on a bed and I was assigned a different physical therapist. Miss Viola Robbins, known as Robbie, was head of the Physical Therapy Department. Having her as a therapist was a mixed blessing. She knew what to do and had the pull to get whatever treatments she thought I needed, but she also had teaching duties. Robbie had the habit of bringing student therapists around to various patients so that the students could observe the therapy sessions. I was the one she picked most of the time, because I was cooperative, and also because I was so thin that my bones, and what muscles I had, were clearly visible. Robbie would come by in the morning, followed by four to six students, ask if I was dressed yet, and proceed with her demonstration. If I said that I was not dressed, she would pull the curtain around the bed. Sometimes, but not always, she would leave the sheet over strategic parts of my body. These were the only concessions to privacy she made. Robbie's physical therapy students were usually female and, more often than not, very attractive. I really liked Robbie, but for a young teenage boy it was very unsettling.

I never complained, because I was taught by my parents not to complain. I also didn't want to blemish my reputation as "the nice, cooperative boy in bed number eight."

I already mentioned the visits by various notables. We were also visited by groups of semi-professional entertainers. These were mostly young girls, between nine and thirteen years old, who would sing or tap dance. Once in a while, some novelty act like a clown or magician would be included. At times there were volunteers from church groups or service organizations, such as the Lions Club or Shriners, who would come in with toys or games for the Children's Ward. There was a Boy Scout troop that came to Rancho for any boys who wanted to participate. I had been a Cub Scout on 109th Street so I thought it would be fun to join. I earned a couple of merit badges, including one for knot tying, while I was still in the iron lung. The scoutmaster would hold a short piece of rope where I could see it, and I would direct him. I would say something like, "Make a loop in the right end of the rope. Now put the left end through the back of the loop, bring it around the right end and back down through the loop again."

The visit that brought the most comment, from both patients and staff, was when my sister came to the hospital in her wedding gown. I was still getting over my cold on the day of the wedding, and the doctors thought it best if I didn't go out. Instead, she came to Rancho to give me an opportunity to see what the gown looked like. The word quickly spread to the other wards, and all of the female patients wanted to see the gown too. Ann went from room to room so that they could get a good look. It was a big hit and was the topic of conversation for several days.

In May 1954, all of the teenagers and younger patients moved to Ward 503. Here my daily activities increased. My tracheostomy was closed, I went to occupational therapy every day, to the pool three times a week, and I was fitted for a pair of leg braces. I could stand and walk a little without braces, but the braces added stability. In June, I received my own wheelchair. For several months, I switched back and forth between using the chair and walking, increasing my walking time until I no longer needed the wheelchair.

Once I could get up, I started writing a journal. I didn't write every day, just when something happened that was worth recording. I had to learn to write with my right hand because my left hand wasn't strong enough to hold a pencil. I wrote a short poem about my new leg braces:

These are my braces,
They set me free.
But, these are my braces,
They are not me.

Without my braces,
I sit in my chair.
Without my braces,
Life is not fair.

But, put on my braces,
And I'm just like the others.
Put on my braces,
And I run like my brothers.

Well, not exactly,
I'll have to admit, no.
Well, not exactly,
'Cause I had polio.

It was obvious by this time that I would have neither the breath nor strength to play the saxophone again. I was very disappointed, but I had to face reality. My parents asked what I wanted to do with it. I suggested they try to sell it. They did, and I got the money from the sale. I felt a little guilty about taking the money. After all, my parents paid for the saxophone originally. I felt guilty, but not guilty enough to refuse the money.

On my trips to therapy I'd meet adults with polio. I knew there were adults at Rancho, but up until then our paths never crossed. The children were in one section and the adults in another. I was a young teenager, but it saddened me to see adults—often mothers and fathers—who could barely move. Who would support the family? Who would take care of their children? We kids got a lot of attention. Everyone felt sorry for "little crippled kids," and gave us a lot of emotional support. But who was going to help the adults?

I was one of the patients who had enough mobility to go to school in the Harriman Building, Rancho's mission-style administration building. Our teacher was Miss Shirley Ludwig. I'm afraid that there were times when we were not the best students. There were too many other things that we liked to do besides study. We'd often take the elevator to the second floor of the Harriman Building and roll down the outside ramps in our wheelchairs. In the evenings, we'd sometimes sneak into the exercise room at the end of 503 and wrestle on the mats. Both activities were frowned on by the staff.

Bill Harber, one of the boys my age, had pretty strong arms but very weak legs. I was just the opposite. I had strong legs, especially my right leg, but weak arms. We'd get down on the exercise mats and "arm" wrestle. He'd use an arm and I'd use my right leg.

Being ambulatory brought other benefits too. I was no longer required to use the bedpan. And, best of all, no more enemas. I had an enema every other day for ten months. Yuch!

Several of the kids on 503 came from out of state. Bill Harber lived in New Mexico and Richard Hakes lived in Arizona. It was difficult for their parents to make frequent visits. Some of the other parents tried to fill this gap, making it a point to visit with them during visiting hours. If their own children asked to have some food from outside the hospital, the parents always asked the "orphaned" kids if they wanted anything special too. Many times the parents were asked to bring hamburgers from the Pow Wow drive-in restaurant or barbecue from the Chris' & Pitt's restaurant.

The last half of 1954 was all pretty much the same: physical therapy, occupational therapy, school, occasional trips to the plaster room for a new body jacket, once a month evaluation of progress with the doctors, etc. I would go home on Friday afternoon and return on Sunday evening. Since nobody was sick, in the usual sense of the word, it was different from what a person might think of as being in a hospital. The main complaints we all had, usually unspoken, were the loss of control over our lives and the lack of privacy. Even at night there were several low-level, indirect lights on. We had no way of knowing when a member of the staff would be walking by our beds.

As teenagers, we were probably more concerned about this than most of the other patients. I remember once when an older teenage couple went out on one of the balconies of the Harriman Building. Someone found them in an amorous embrace. It was something that would be quite ordinary on the "outside world," but some of the hospital staff threw a fit. Dr. Wendland, the staff psychologist, had to intervene on the couple's behalf. He finally convinced those who were most disturbed that they had over-reacted.

That sort of thing didn't happen very often, but there was one head nurse on the afternoon shift who acted a lot like a prison warden, at least in my opinion. She seemed to have two rules. Rule number one was, "Patients should do exactly as told." Rule number two was, "Everything else is forbidden."

It helped to pass the time if you had a good imagination. The ceilings on the wards had random patterns built into them. As I lay in bed, I would look at the ceiling and conjure up images of things I pretended to build: a go-cart, a rocket ship, a house. Mentally working on different house plans took quite a bit of my free time. Sometimes I would conjure up images of female body parts.

My muscles didn't work very well but my hormones sure did. After all, I was a teenage boy. In that respect I was no different from other boys my age. The only real difference was that I lived in a hospital. Most boys could arrange their own privacy. They could lock the bathroom door, or at least expect to be left alone when they were in their beds at night. They wouldn't usually have trouble finding a place to sneak a peek at "girly magazines," or find a private time to do what teenage boys do. My problem was that I would wake up in the middle of the night on the verge of another wet dream. Sometimes I would go back to sleep, hoping to continue the dream, and hoping the dream would lead to the inevitable. Of course, that would pose other embarrassing problems. But at those times you're usually not thinking beyond the moment. In addition to living in a hospital, my options were limited by the weakness of my upper extremities, especially when lying down. I had difficulty doing what teenage boys do.

℞ ℞ ℞ ℞ ℞

As the end of 1954 approached, I learned that I would be sent home on a trial basis. Between Christmas and New Year's Day, I was put in a solid body jacket. By solid, I mean that it could not be removed. Normally a body jacket has buckles in front so you can take it off to bathe. On December 31, 1954, I was discharged and given an appointment to the Outpatient Clinic for the following March. I returned once during that time when I tripped and fell, hitting the driveway cement and knocking out one of my front teeth.

One afternoon, during my three month hiatus from Rancho, I was watching a cooking show on television. The guest chef, Philip Harben, was from England. After his cooking segment, he talked about life in Great Britain and demonstrated a game that was played in many pubs. The game was called Table Skittles, and combined the skills of tether ball and bowling in a large tabletop game. My mother was sitting nearby, and I casually remarked, "Even I could play that."

I didn't give the game much thought after my offhand remark, but my mother obviously did. Sometime later that day she called the office of the British Consul-General in Los Angeles, and asked if they knew where the game could be purchased in southern California. I wasn't aware of the conversation, but evidently the Consul-General saw an opportunity for good public relations. He came to our house the next day, accompanied by a reporter and photographer from the *Los Angeles Times*. The Consul-General presented me with the same game that Philip Harben had used for his demonstration on television. He also gave me a signed copy of Harben's book *The Young Cook*. My picture and the story appeared on the inside front page of the paper the following day. It must have been a very slow news day.

℞ ℞ ℞ ℞ ℞

In March 1955, I returned to the Outpatient Clinic and had my body jacket cut off. Having casts cut off was never one of my favorite activities. In theory the saw is designed to cut hard objects like plaster and leave soft things like skin alone. But when you are as thin as I was, the theory didn't always work. The saw couldn't tell the difference between the cast and my hipbones, ankles, or any other bony point of my body. I usually looked like I had walked through barbed wire when I left the plaster room.

With the cast off, it was obvious that body jackets were not going to keep my back from getting progressively more crooked. I was sent home to have the three-month accumulation of crud washed off my upper body and told to report to the next Scoliosis Clinic. It was decided at that time that I should be readmitted to Rancho.

I re-entered Rancho on March 22, 1955. Because of my scoliosis, the doctors gave orders that I was to remain flat on my back, at least until they could decide what to do next. While at home I had a physical therapist who came twice a week to put me through range of motion exercises. These continued in the hospital and, in addition, a different therapist started me on a series of back-stretching sessions. The two therapists would put me face down on a work table and slide my body off one end. One of them held my hips flat to the table while the other bent my head and shoulders down and to the side. Several people said it looked like they were torturing me but, actually, it hurt very little. Maybe my pain threshold was just high.

I spent the first couple of weeks on Ward 501. I was in bed when we learned of the successful field trials of Dr. Jonas Salk's polio vaccine. Those of us who had enough breathing capacity to shout "Hooray" certainly did. No sane person would want another human joining our exclusive "club." Our club has pretty awful initiation rituals and continuing "dues" of pain, struggle, and frustration.

I heard only one sour grapes comment. A man in his early twenties said, "Yeah, you're a little late, guy." Other than this, I seldom heard any complaints from patients. Of course, the younger patients sometimes cried when therapy hurt, but they usually dried their eyes and resumed play with the others when therapy was over. I couldn't read anybody's mind, and it would be expected that some patients had episodes of anger or despair, but I saw few outward signs of this.

My stay on 501 was just temporary. A decision had been made to put all the teenage patients in their own area. When space became available, we went to Ward 502. There were never more than six boys, and even fewer girls, in an area designed for sixteen patients. We had plenty of room. Things were much less structured here than on previous wards. As long as we were where we were supposed to be for therapy or meals, we were pretty much free to do what we wanted. We still had school, of course, and some unscheduled activities. Because I was confined to bed, except for physical therapy sessions, I didn't get to take advantage of this new freedom right away. But it wasn't too long before I was fitted with another body jacket and allowed to get back up.

We spent most of our free time in the solarium or having wheelchair races in the halls. I pushed my chair backwards, using my right foot. One of the resident physicians, Dr. Hiscock, kept his office door open most of the time. He issued a standing invitation to come in and ask questions or look through his medical books. We would go through his copy of *Gray's Anatomy* to find some obscure part of the human body and ask each other if anybody could tell where it was located. I had good success with "corocoid process" and "Poupart's ligament." I probably learned more about anatomy and physiology than most kids my age.

Another of our favorite projects was seeing how much free literature we could get. We sent for information on all sorts of subjects and from all sorts of places. We requested pamphlets and brochures from such diverse sources as the American Petroleum Institute, the United States Printing Office, and Planned Parenthood. The Planned Parenthood packet brought some raised eyebrows from the hospital staff. The package of information on sex and birth control had obviously been opened by someone before it got to us. Some staff person was probably trying to protect us from the evils of the outside world. We always used my address: Richard Daggett, %502D, Rancho Los Amigos.

Rancho had its own small newspaper. It was usually two or three mimeographed pages containing human interest stories about the patients and staff. It was published by the patients and came out weekly. They called it, very appropriately, the *Weakly Breather.* In one issue, as a joke, one of the contributing writers included an article about me. It congratulated me and said I was finally going home to be with, "my wife and two kids."

We even had a yearly beauty/popularity contest. We elected a "Miss Breathless," a "Mr. Breathless," and a "Little Whisper." Usually some celebrity was asked to come and crown the winners. Ronald Reagan was one of those who came.

$$\text{\textit{⌒⌒ ⌒⌒ ⌒⌒ ⌒⌒ ⌒⌒}}$$

During the summer months, I had several appointments at the Scoliosis Clinic. Usually Dr. Vernon Nickel, chief of the Orthopedic Service, would have the doctors look on as he described the patient's history. Then he would ask for recommendations concerning possible treatments. It seemed that in my case they always said, "Operate!" In preparation for this, I was ordered to have a complete set of x-rays: front, back, side, standing, and lying down. I also had a series of photographs taken. Karen Whitaker, a girl on our ward, had photographs taken at the same time. To say it was embarrassing for both of us would be an understatement. I was just a month past my fifteenth birthday and Karen was about six months younger. We were together in this small room, wearing nothing but very loose, loincloth things, with strings at the corners that were tied around our waist. They hung loosely between our legs, and only covered our private parts if you were looking straight at us. Karen also had what appeared to be a small piece of ace bandage that was supposed to cover her breasts. It didn't do a very good job and she knew it. I could tell by her expression that it bothered her a lot. I must admit that I peeked a little while she was having her pictures taken. Karen must have peeked at me too. I overheard her later that day telling another girl, "The way Richard was standing I could see almost everything." For a couple of days Karen and I had trouble looking at each other face to face. I don't know why they didn't take our photographs separately. I guess it was an example of institutional insensitivity that was common in the 1950s and earlier. The photographer told us that he would put black spots over our faces and that nobody but the doctors would see the photographs. Maybe that was the plan, but I saw them a few days later, and I'm guessing others might have seen them too. Our friends on the ward obviously knew what happened and kidded us for days about the "nude" photographs.

I hadn't had an opportunity to see my whole body since contracting polio and it was pretty discouraging to see these photographs. I think I was about nine or ten years old when I first became aware of my physical appearance. It bothered me that I could never seem to develop a tan, and I thought I looked rather soft and puny. I wasn't, but that's how I felt. Then, just before my polio onset at age thirteen, I looked in the mirror and saw the development of muscles and the beginnings of a potential adult. Now here I was, fifteen years old and almost literally nothing but skin and bones. It was a real blow to my ego. It was obvious that I had matured physically, which was a little bit of a surprise in itself, because I hadn't seen myself naked since I was barely thirteen years old. I had the usual secondary sex characteristics—adult genitals and pubic and underarm hair—but I also looked like a corpse of a person who had died from malnutrition. It reminded me of the pictures taken of bodies in the World War II concentration camps. I was fifteen years old, five feet nine inches tall, and I weighed barely ninety pounds.

I happened to see these photographs again, many years later, and I was given a copy recently by hospital staff. I'm still thin, and in some ways more visibly disabled than I was in 1955, but I hope I've filled out a little bit.

Another embarrassing thing happened about that same time. It seems funny looking back, but it wasn't then. I had to fill out a psychological questionnaire for one of Dr. Wendland's projects. It happened that I was immobilized with casts, so one of the teen volunteers offered to help. She would read the questions to me and fill in my answers. Most of the questions were rather mundane, like "What is your favorite color?" or "What animal would you like to be if you weren't human?" It worked fine until she came to a series of very personal questions about my sexual experiences and fantasies. I remember thinking, "I'm fifteen years old and I live in a hospital. What kind of sexual experiences do they *think* I've had?" Even if I'd had any real sexual experiences it would have been too embarrassing to tell them to the attractive girl sitting beside my bed. After several awkward moments we made it to the end. It would have made a great Woody Allen comedy sketch.

About this same time I was asked to be a kind of living "dummy." I would go to the various physical therapy classes when they wanted to demonstrate why a patient might benefit from some therapy they were discussing. It was an extension of what Robbie did with me on the wards.

One of the things unique to my situation was that even on weekend passes I couldn't completely escape the hospital environment. Dr. Nickel lived down the street from us, just three houses away. I would be home, standing in the front yard, when he would walk down the street or ride by on his bicycle. Dr. Nickel was a great orthopedic surgeon, but he was never my favorite person. He almost always had a scowl on his face and, when he would see me, he appeared to be sizing me up for some new therapy or corrective surgery.

For two months I heard very little about any possible surgery on my back. Then, late in September, a lady came to me on the ward, handed me a clipboard with a piece of paper, and said, "Sign this!" I didn't read the whole thing but it looked like an authorization for surgery. I signed it, but I'm not sure why they wanted my signature. I was only fifteen years old.

The next day I was sent to the plaster room where I was once more hoisted up on the rack for a new cast. All of the previous body casts had gone from my hips to my underarms. This one went from my knees to the top of my head. There were holes left in the cast: one over my stomach area so that I could breathe easier, others in the front and back so that I could use a bedpan or urinal, and, of course, my face was left exposed. A couple of days later I went back and had the cast sawed off. They cut along both sides of my body so that the cast was separated into two parts. It was designed so that I could lie in the bottom part and the top would fit over me, sort of like the lid of a tight-fitting sarcophagus.

The whole sawing process was extremely unpleasant. Besides the usual cuts and scratches, it was just about the loudest noise I'd ever heard. The plaster was covering my ears and it amplified the sound of the saw, especially as it neared my head.

The surgery was scheduled for October 11, 1955, and I was sent to the surgery ward a couple of days before. I had what I considered an unnecessarily large blood sample taken by a man who kept poking away until he got what he wanted. My back was washed with a strong disinfectant and other preparations were made.

They doped me up pretty well the morning of the operation. I was wheeled into surgery and saw Dr. Nickel and Dr. Jacquelin Perry. I vaguely remember someone feeling my arm and asking for an 18 gauge needle. In my sedated state it sounded to me like he asked for a needle eighteen inches long. I thought, "Where could they put a needle eighteen inches long in my body that wouldn't stick out the other side?" If I had been able, I would have run out of the operating room so fast nobody would have been able to catch me.

My spinal fusion was done in two stages. They took small chips of bone from the sides of my vertebrae and used them to plaster over the joints, effectively fusing them together. In the first operation, they fused the third through the eighth thoracic vertebrae. This first operation went well. Except for the first couple of days there was very little discomfort. I was put in a tank respirator as a precaution, but was back on the bed and into my sarcophagus cast in three days. The fourth day I was back on Ward 502. About two weeks after surgery they took the stitches out. No problem at all.

Three weeks after the first operation, I was back on the surgery ward being prepared for the second stage. Things just didn't seem to go right this time. I was taken up to surgery about eight in the morning, but there had been a scheduling mix-up and I had to go back down to the surgery ward to wait. I finally got into the operating room about eleven o'clock. By then the sedatives had worn off. I was wide awake as they slid me onto the table and began hooking me up to various tubes and bottles. It was a relief to hear somebody say, "Put him under." This time they fused the ninth thoracic through the third lumber vertebrae.

When it came time to remove this second set of stitches, it was about the worst pain I had ever experienced. My skin had grown over the tops of the stitches and two doctors worked about forty minutes digging the stitches out. I had some things done to me at General Hospital that really hurt, like the spinal tap and the cut down, but this was much worse. Excruciating is the only word that comes to mind. I tried not to make a sound but I'm sure a few muffled moans escaped, and I'm afraid a few tears escaped too. Richard Hakes, the boy in the bed next to me, said later, "That must've really hurt. They've done some pretty tough stuff to you but this was the first time I ever heard a peep out of you."

After my incision had healed sufficiently, they sealed the sarcophagus cast closed. I was sent home, cast and all, the day before Thanksgiving 1955. My father made a wheeled platform for me to lie on. I spent most of the time in the living room, watching TV or reading. A teacher came to the house and gave me my school assignments.

I returned to the Outpatient Clinic in March 1956 and the long cast was removed. X-rays were taken of my spine and a short body jacket-type cast was put on. After being sealed in for almost four months from the top of my head to my knees, it sure felt good to move around. And boy, was I a mess! My hair was all matted, and dead skin rolled off everywhere. It took days to get clean. A couple of months later the short cast was removed. Now I really was free. I was still crooked, but I was stable. I could stand under the shower and let the water run all over me. It was wonderful!

With the short cast removed, I was officially discharged from the hospital. I continued to see Dr. Nickel for several months as a private patient, and I had private physical therapy sessions with Bob Kaplan, a Rancho physical therapist who also had an office in Whittier. My mother drove me to Whittier twice a week, and on the way home we usually stopped at McDonald's for a cheeseburger and chocolate malt. This McDonald's is in Downey, at the corner of Florence Avenue and Lakewood Boulevard. It is still there, is the oldest McDonald's remaining in operation, and has the original golden arches design.

Moving On

I continued school with a home teacher. In those days, students with a disability were not encouraged to attend regular classes. There were some differences in the courses offered to me too, although it might have been just a peculiarity of my teachers. Course requirements included "Senior Problems," a mixture of things that included a mild form of sex education called "Family Life." My teacher said of Family Life, "We can skip this if you want. I'm sure you know it anyway, and you'll probably never need it." I was too polite to tell him he was showing his ignorance about people with disabilities. He probably thought, like many people do, that if a person is disabled he or she loses any interest in sexual matters. The funny thing is, another course requirement was driver education. Although it was very unlikely that I would ever have the upper body strength to drive, he still made me take the textbook part of driver education. He probably felt more comfortable teaching me how to drive than he did talking to me about sex.

I know I benefited academically by having a home teacher, but my social life surely suffered. My neighborhood friends would come over occasionally, and I was invited to a few parties, but not very often. I was, however, getting very good grades. I had always gotten good grades in Reading, English, Art, and Social Studies, but only acceptable in Math. I still struggled with Algebra, but Geometry and Trigonometry were a snap. And having a teacher on a one-to-one basis meant I couldn't fake it. If I was having a problem with a certain subject, the teacher knew it immediately. Overall, it was probably good for me. But I missed taking science lab courses and mixing with the other students.

I already mentioned my lack of an outside social life. This was compounded by the social rituals of the time. In the 1950s, it was the young man's responsibility to provide for transportation and to pay for meals and entertainment. I didn't drive, and I had very little income of my own. And not attending school meant I knew very few girls my age.

I probably had a pretty low physical self-image too. I was well-liked and felt at ease with individuals or in small groups, but I was uncomfortable in many situations. This was especially true when I was around girls whom I had known before I contracted polio. I remember once when Jeannette Roulon came to our door soliciting donations or selling something. I had a severe crush on Jeannette in the seventh grade. My mother knew her and invited her in. I was mortified. I was lying on the couch, in pajama bottoms and a t-shirt. I must have looked like an animated, half-dressed skeleton. At least that's how I felt. We exchanged a few words and she left. I sensed that Jeannette was just as embarrassed as I was. I was angry with my mother for not giving me some warning, and I pledged to myself that I would never be caught in that situation again. From the time I got out of bed in the morning until the time I went to bed at night I was fully dressed. I wore my leg braces, long pants, and a long-sleeve shirt.

There is a stereotype of a teenager looking into a mirror and saying, "I can't go out tonight. I've got this great big zit on my face." They think that everyone is going to be staring at their pimple. I was seldom troubled by acne, but walking with braces and having limited use of my upper extremities, I sometimes felt that everyone in the room was watching me. It took many, many years for me to overcome this.

While I was in the tenth grade, the school district made a decision that home students would not be able to take a full course load. Whatever their reasoning, and I did not agree with it, this meant that I would not graduate until 1959. One benefit to this, however, was that I got to graduate with the first graduating class from the newly-built Warren High School. I had never actually been on campus, except for a basketball game, but a few days before the graduation ceremony I attended a school assembly. I was recognized for academic achievement by the California Scholastic Federation.

& & & & &

In my senior year, a friend of mine from our neighborhood got married. He came to visit a few days before the ceremony and seemed depressed. He confirmed what I had guessed. He was getting married because his girlfriend was pregnant. He told me that they were in love, and he wasn't sorry he was marrying her, but he was afraid they were getting married too young. He was my age and she was a year younger. During our conversation he said, "If you ever get the opportunity, don't." He meant that if I ever had the opportunity to have intercourse, I shouldn't do it. He felt that the pleasure he got from sex wasn't worth the trouble he was in now. As we talked, I began to feel kind of depressed myself. I was thinking, "I wear braces on my legs. My arms are weak. My body is terribly thin and crooked. I don't look even remotely desirable. It is very unlikely that any girl would ever want to have a sexual relationship with me." In fact, about the only parts of my body that worked the way they were supposed to were my brain and my reproductive system, and now my friend was telling me that even if someone wanted to have a sexual relationship with me, I shouldn't let it happen! After the wedding, my friend seemed to be in great spirits. His happiness should have made me pleased, but it didn't. It just made me more aware of our different situations. Being sexually active doesn't define a person as a man, or even as an adult. But, feeling that a sexual relationship is beyond your reach is very frustrating.

Does my lack of sexual expression make me less than fully human? Priests and nuns make that choice. And, historically, there have been entire communities that have made the choice to be celibate. The defining word here is "choice." This is probably true, even in my case. Being disabled was not my choice, but I have a few severely disabled friends who made the choice, despite their disability, to marry or enter into intimate relationships. So, in reality, the choice was there for me too. The fear of rejection probably clouded my choices.

Several months after graduating from high school, the California Department of Rehabilitation asked me to take a series of scholastic and aptitude tests. These were designed to evaluate my employment potential and direct any future academic pursuits. I was surprised that I did so well. I say I was surprised, because I'd always had the nagging feeling that my home teachers were fudging a little on my grades. The thought crossed my mind, more than once, that I was getting very good grades because the teachers felt sorry for me. The lady giving these tests said that I scored in the upper 25 percent of college freshman, overall, and in the upper 10 percent when compared to engineering students. My IQ was 131, well into the superior range. It took a while before I really believed this. I think the lady sensed my disbelief, because she gave me a copy of her written report, saying she didn't usually do this.

Because I graduated from high school with honors, and because I had done well on these scholastic and aptitude tests, I was urged to consider college. I did consider it, but I had many internal conflicts to resolve. Schools in the 1950s, including colleges, didn't encourage attendance by students with my degree of disability. This was slowly changing, but many obstacles remained. Although I could walk, and climb most stairs, I had trouble opening doors. And I couldn't take notes very well, so college lectures would be a problem. Even getting back and forth to classes would be very difficult. I also had to give thought to personal hygiene. I could urinate by myself, but I had to have help wiping if I had a bowel movement. This problem wasn't solved until the late 1970s, when I had a toilet seat bidet installed. And this solution worked only at home.

I also had a real fear of catching a respiratory infection. It seemed that two or three times a year my brother Robert would come home from college with a cold or sore throat. I am no more susceptible to colds than the next person, but if I do get one it is almost always difficult for me. A cold usually puts me out of commission for a week or two. This was a psychological barrier that I found hard to overcome.

The third reason was probably a bit selfish. I enjoyed the trips I took with my parents. If I enrolled in college full time, I would not be able to participate in these. And, knowing my parents, they would probably curtail their traveling to help me. I think I would have enjoyed most aspects of college life, but I'm not sorry I made the choice I did.

In the late fifties and early sixties, I took several college level courses through UCLA Extension. Not for credit, but for my own enjoyment. I took several units of History and a number of science courses, including Physics, Geology, Biology, Physiology, and Psychology. I've done this on an occasional basis ever since. I've enjoyed these academic challenges and they have given me insights into the world around me. Still, it would be nice to have a college diploma to hang on the wall.

In 1958, we sold my father's home-made trailer and bought a fifteen-foot, commercially made trailer. We traveled in this rig to western Canada in 1958 and to Colorado in 1960. On both of these trips we were joined by the Sperry family. We usually made a couple of trips a year to Yosemite National Park too. When we were traveling in areas where radio reception was limited, we could almost always pick up station KSL out of Salt Lake, Utah. This was one of the few stations that had a strong, clear signal. We would often listen to the Mormon Tabernacle Choir on Sunday mornings. One of my favorite hymns is the Mormon "Come, Come Ye Saints," sometimes known as "All is Well."

It was on one of these trailer trips that I first began experimenting with a mustache. I didn't shave for about a week, then shaved off my whiskers in stages, leaving long sideburns and a mustache, and finally just the mustache. I've done this on other trips too, ending with a different configuration each time.

In preparation for our trip to Canada I bought a twenty-power spotting scope that could be attached to the camera. I've taken some interesting pictures with this setup, but I usually used the scope by itself. I would often set it on a tripod in a mountain meadow, or on a bluff at the beach, and watch the birds and animals. Sometimes humans would be doing things that were interesting. Once I had the scope set up in the middle of a meadow near El Capitan, in Yosemite

National Park. We were watching some men climb up the face of this sheer rock wall. They appeared to be having trouble and, after a few minutes, a huge military helicopter landed in the meadow not far from us. As they made preparations to rescue the climbers, a very large crowd gathered. Everyone wanted to take a look through the scope. If I had charged admission, I could have made a small fortune.

Late in 1959, my sister's son Steven began staying with us during the day while his mother was at work. He was about three years old. Steve would come in the door in the morning and say to me, "What are we going to do today?" I often took him on bug hunts around our yard.

Steve was a well-behaved, good-natured little boy. I had to be resourceful the few times he misbehaved. I knew there was no way I could chase him down and paddle his behind, so I decided to use a little psychological warfare. If he acted up, I told him to stop or I wouldn't talk to him until he mended his ways. If he persisted, I made good on my promise. My silent treatment usually lasted only a half hour or so. It always did the trick. I also helped babysit my other nephews and niece. One or two at a time was enjoyable, but much more than that was a little hectic.

On September 28, 1961, as I was watering the front lawn, I began having some severe chest pains. I went to see Dr. Hershey at the Ross-Loos Clinic. He didn't think it was my heart but thought further tests should be done. It was arranged that I enter Rancho again. The doctors in residence took several EKGs that didn't really prove anything. To be on the safe side, they put me in a tank respirator overnight. It was almost like returning to the womb. I fell asleep within minutes and slept soundly until the morning, not even waking for dinner. A tank respirator might be confining, but it is quite comfortable.

The next day I had another EKG. The pains slowly subsided. During the week I was there I had two more EKGs, several x-rays, and some tests to check the carbon dioxide (CO_2) level in my blood.

CO_2 is a normal component of blood, along with oxygen, but too much CO_2 can interfere with the blood's ability to carry oxygen.

It seemed like a dozen doctors listened to my chest, but it is still a mystery as to what caused the pains. My own theory is that it had something to do with an impending cold, because the day I left Rancho I came down with a real rip-snorter.

Rancho had really changed since I left in 1956. The 500 Wards were all polio patients when I lived there. Now there were hardly any, at least there weren't many where I was. Most patients had spinal cord injuries or had a variety of other ailments. The man in the bed next to me had a collapsed lung. Two beds away was a man with what seemed to be the delirium tremens. He kept us awake all night. The lady on the other side of him didn't look like she had anything wrong. Just her presence was new to me. Coed wards were unheard of when I was a patient. Five years had made a big difference in staff too. I met some nurses and attendants who I knew from before, but most of the personnel had changed. One of the nursing attendants on the evening shift had been a teen volunteer in 1955. She was the same one who helped me fill out the infamous psychological questionnaire! We had a good laugh about that.

Upon leaving, I was given an appointment for the Outpatient Clinic. At the clinic I was sent for another EKG and another CO_2 test. My CO_2 level was a little high, so I was issued a Thompson Zephyr. This is a positive pressure machine that I used for chest stretching and to augment my cough if I had a cold. The doctors wanted to keep tabs on my CO_2 level, so I began regular, twice-a-year visits to the Outpatient Clinic.

$\sim\!\!\sim$ $\sim\!\!\sim$ $\sim\!\!\sim$ $\sim\!\!\sim$ $\sim\!\!\sim$

1962 was a big year. My father retired from Western Electric, we sold our house on Wiley-Burke, put our furniture in storage, and bought a new Buick and a new twenty-five foot Airstream "Land Yacht." The Airstream would be our home for the next year and a half. A twenty-five foot trailer is a little small for three people, but since we were traveling a lot of the time we managed quite well.

Our first trip was to Seattle, Washington. This was the year of the Seattle World's Fair. We saw all the major pavilions, ate dinner at the top of the Space Needle, and watched a really terrific show that evening. It was Canada Week at the fair and the Canadian military put on a "Military Tattoo," which combines the traditional sounds of bagpipes and drums with other aspects of the armed forces.

We spent most of the winter of 1962 in the Southern California desert, in Palm Springs and Anza Borrego State Park. After Christmas, we rented a space in a trailer park in Downey. My father needed some surgery and we had to have a place to stay for his recuperation.

By April 1963, he had returned to health and we decided to attend the Airstream International Rally to be held that year in Bemidji, Minnesota. Over the next few weeks we traveled through Arizona, New Mexico, Texas, Oklahoma, Arkansas, Missouri, and Illinois. We arranged to meet our Airstream friends, Athlone and Gene Gwaltney, in Springfield, Illinois.

After a few days visit we left, agreeing to meet them again in Fond du Lac, Wisconsin. We headed north to Chicago, east to Detroit, and then north again over the Straits of Mackinac. We traveled along the southern shore of Lake Superior, and then south to Fond du Lac. The Gwaltneys had lived in Fond du Lac for many years and were able to show us all the points of interest in that part of Wisconsin.

We joined the International Rally on June 17, 1963. This was sponsored by the Airstream company and the Wally Byam Caravan Club, International. The Wally Byam Caravan Club is an association of Airstream owners. About three thousand shiny Airstream trailers filled the Bemidji fairgrounds. The club arranged for people attending the rally to change some of their money into two-dollar bills. This way, when we would shop in towns in the vicinity, the local merchants could see the benefits of having an Airstream rally in the area. We also wore our Wally Byam blue berets whenever we were with our group.

After the rally we joined about three hundred and fifty trailer families on the Airstream Eastern Canada Caravan. We spent six weeks visiting the Canadian Provinces of Ontario, Quebec, New Brunswick, Prince Edward Island, and Nova Scotia. It was one of the most interesting and enjoyable times I've ever had.

When the caravan ended in September, we traveled a leisurely, meandering course down the east coast of the United States. We would go inland a few hundred miles, then return to points of interest on the coast. We had exceptionally good weather and the fall colors were a treat for us. My only regret is that I didn't know then about our Daggett ancestors who had lived in New England. I knew that my great-grandfather, James Monroe Daggett, was born in Maine and had been in the Maine Volunteers during the Civil War. And I had seen a book in the Los Angeles Central Library giving information about the first Daggetts to come to America in 1630. This book listed one of the descendants as Robert Daggett of Maine. Unfortunately, there was a gap in the information contained in this book and the knowledge I had then of our family's history. I learned several years later that Robert Daggett was the father of James Monroe Daggett. It would have been interesting to visit the towns where these very early Daggetts had lived.

By November, we had reached Florida. We spent a week in Palm Beach, and while there we met President Kennedy, who was visiting his ailing father. Ten days later we were in Tampa when we heard of his assassination. We were probably among the first to hear this sad news. We were in the Tampa police station, trying to find the address of my mother's uncle who lived in the area, when the news of the assassination came over the police teletype.

We had planned to take a leisurely month to return to California but this took the wind out of our sails. We headed west, stopping to have Thanksgiving dinner with Airstream friends in Houston and to tour Carlsbad Caverns. Other than these two stops, our daily drives were pretty somber. We arrived home the first week of December. We had been gone from home for more than eight months, and had traveled considerably more than 23,000 miles.

My father and I took hundreds and hundreds of 35mm slides on this trip. As we finished each roll we sent it in to be processed. Most of them were waiting for us when we arrived back in southern California. As we sorted them and prepared to catalog them I saw a photograph my father had taken eight months earlier. It was a photograph of downtown Dallas, Texas. In the middle of the picture is Dealy Plaza and the Texas School Book Depository; the building where Lee Harvey Oswald fired at President Kennedy. It sent a chill down my spine.

⁶⁶ ⁶⁶ ⁶⁶ ⁶⁶ ⁶⁶

After Christmas, we began to look for another home. We started by looking at a number of mobile homes. The idea of low maintenance appealed to us, but renting a space in a mobile home park did not. Even those areas where you could buy your own lot had many of the elements of rental.

Our search for a place to settle covered most of southern California, from inland San Diego County to Santa Barbara County. We finally decided on another house in Downey. We bought our home on La Reina in March 1964.

⁶⁶ ⁶⁶ ⁶⁶ ⁶⁶ ⁶⁶

Since 1961, I have returned to the Rancho Outpatient Clinic on a regular basis. Several times I have gone to Rancho, on request, to help in testing or to do my living dummy routine when they needed a model. Over the years, I have also actively participated in several studies conducted on issues relating to disability. Most were conducted at Rancho, while others were conducted by contacts I had made at Rancho. One of the most interesting was on bio-technical research. A panel of engineers asked us about how we used various household appliances, and how they could be designed differently to meet the specific needs of a person with a disability.

It was an interesting study, and I enjoyed participating in it, but I'm not sure we were of much help. The engineers appeared to have a concept of disability that didn't match reality. Their preconceptions limited them to a single view of disability and few of us fit that stereotype.

Another very interesting study was on the sexual aspects of living with a disability. My friend Justin Laird also took part in the study. I acted as the resource person and was given a list of literature and audio-visual materials the sponsors thought would be helpful. I was asked to locate these materials and try to buy or rent them at reduced rates. It was surprising to me that I was successful most of the time. One offshoot of the study was that I got on a lot of unusual mailing lists. I still get some mail that would probably shock many people. I was also able to keep many of the books and pamphlets relating to adolescent sexual development, and I've often shared these with friends who have children.

This program was part of a larger study to compare psychological differences and sexual response patterns between various population groups. In our case, the research team wanted to determine how living through adolescence in an institutional setting would affect sexual responses and attitudes. The study showed that most of the participants, both disabled and non-disabled, were similar. The only real difference was that those who spent lengthy periods in institutional settings during childhood and adolescence had a much more rapid response to sexual stimuli. No doubt because a person doesn't get much "sexual stimuli" living in an institution.

Justin was my best friend. We had many things in common. Besides our obvious polio experiences we had very similar childhood backgrounds. Our fathers both worked for the same company, and we shared many social and political beliefs. After the sexuality study, we often kidded each other about our lack of sexual experience. I think our kidding was a way to mask our true frustrations and disappointments about this.

    *   *   *   *   *

In 1964, the CO_2 level in my blood began to rise again and it was decided that I should use a portable chest shell respirator at night, at least part of the time. It was similar to the one I used as I was transitioning away from the tank respirator in 1953. My CO_2 level stabilized and the doctors did not seem overly concerned.

Using this respirator setup didn't stop our travels. We took it along on our 1965 trip to western Canada. This was again with our Wally Byam Caravan Club. We drove north through Grand Teton and Yellowstone National Parks, then to the International Rally in Laramie, Wyoming. About four thousand Airstream trailers were parked on the University of Wyoming grounds. After the rally, we gathered for the Airstream Western Canada Caravan at Williston, North Dakota. It was large caravan of about four hundred trailers. We entered Canada through Saskatchewan and toured Alberta and British Columbia. Some of our stopping places in the Canadian Rockies were really spectacular. About four hundred shiny trailers parked in a valley between steep, glacier covered peaks is a sight to behold. We were gone from home about three months.

Over the years, we had traveled to so many interesting places, and along so many beautiful roads, that I decided to make a record of our various routes. I took a North American highway atlas and used an orange felt tip marker to highlight the roads we had traveled. I decided not to mark California roads because we've been on so many of them that the whole state map would have been colored orange.

As I write this I've tried to think of my favorite drives. State Highway 1, on the California coast has to be near the top of this list. But, so do many others: the "Avenue of the Giants" through the redwoods; parts of Highway 101 on the Oregon coast; the highway going between Jasper and Banff in the Canadian Rockies; the road through Tuolumne Meadows in Yosemite; the drive around Cape Breton Highlands in Nova Scotia; the drive down the Blue Ridge Parkway, especially in the fall. I could fill pages with this list.

Often when we were traveling I would look at a map of the local area and find some minor rural road to explore. We made it a habit to seek out these routes. Once, when we were traveling with friends, they jokingly accused me of routing us over every crooked road in the vicinity. We've been on many roads that only a small percentage of travelers see. Probably not one in ten thousand visitors to Yellowstone National Park took the then-unpaved Old Tower Falls Road. A similar percentage of visitors to Death Valley National Monument take the road down Titus Canyon, and even fewer drive up to Aguerreberry Point. Probably not one in a million visitors to the Copper Harbor area of northern Michigan drive on the really primitive road to the very tip of Keweenaw Peninsula, jutting out into Lake Superior. Some of these drives were an adventure, and all were rewarding.

Ever since we joined the Wally Byam Caravan Club, our local Long Beach Unit officers had tried to get my father to serve on the board. He always turned them down. Even my mother and I tried to talk him into it. One evening, after our monthly dinner meeting, the president came over to our table and asked to speak to him. I assumed the president was going to ask him to serve on the board again. As my father was getting up from our table I said, "Whatever he wants, say yes." When my father returned he had a sheepish grin. I asked him what the president had wanted. He reminded me that I had urged him to say yes, so he did. But what the president had asked was if my father thought I would be willing to serve as recording secretary. My father laughed and said, "You told me to say yes." I guess I tricked myself into the job. I also took over the duties of Unit Reporter for the *Blue Beret*, the Airstream national publication. This was the start of my involvement with journalism.

If, during my high school years, someone had asked me what occupation I was leaning toward, journalism would have been pretty far down the list. I could write a school report but it was always "homework," in the drudgery sense of the word. As I wrote my articles for the *Blue Beret*, I discovered that, not only was I pretty good at it, I actually enjoyed putting sentences on paper in a logical order. I struggle with it sometimes, but I get real satisfaction when things fall into place.

2∞ 2∞ 2∞ 2∞ 2∞

Our family has always attended church. We went to the Inglewood Methodist Church when I was young and the First Methodist Church at 8th and Hope in downtown Los Angeles from 1948 to 1951. We joined the Downey Methodist Church in 1951. The Downey church presented a mild culture shock to me in the beginning. The First Methodist Church in downtown Los Angeles had been very large and very formal. The minister, J. Richard Snead, had a deep, booming voice. To a child it was almost as if God himself was preaching.

The Downey church was very different. At that time the sanctuary was a medium-size structure and appeared typical of small-town America. The minister, Francis Cook, was very friendly and looked like someone you might see driving a tractor. There were several older men who sat together on the front pew and would shout "Amen!" or "Hallelujah!" during the sermon. This was a new experience for me.

My mother was active in the various women's groups of the church, but I was what you might call a "Sunday morning Methodist." I attended Sunday school classes when I was young, then regular

Sunday morning worship services as an adult. The link between Sunday mornings and church was seldom broken. Even when traveling, we often attended a local church.

In the mid-1970s, I began to get active in several church activities. I helped in the church office at least one day a week and substituted for the secretary when she was on vacation. One Sunday morning my father and I were attending a Methodist Men's breakfast. Loren Grandey, the immediate past president, asked if I would consider serving on the Methodist Men's board. I could think of no reason for declining, except for the fact that I didn't drive. He said that transportation could be provided, so I agreed to serve. Little did I know where this would lead.

It turned out that the board members served as president, in rotation, and eventually it became my turn. The Men's Club president was required to represent the Club on the church Administrative Council. I also had to preside at the breakfast meetings and arrange for speakers. This brought me to the attention of our minister, Norris Barnes. He asked me to be the liturgist during the Sunday morning worship service. I had spoken to groups before, but standing at the lectern in front of the whole congregation was a challenge. I was nervous, but I figured these were all my friends and even if I made a mistake no one was going to throw rotten fruit at me. Actually, I wasn't too bad, and I served in this capacity a number of times.

Later I became the church's historian. I wrote a history of the Downey church and chaired our sesquicentennial celebration in 2004. The Downey United Methodist Church is one of the oldest in southern California.

I received a wonderful surprise for my fortieth birthday. My sister Ann secretly arranged for us to ride in the Goodyear blimp. We were going to my Uncle Arthur's funeral in the afternoon, but we left the house at mid-morning. I wondered why we had left the house so early, and why we were driving in the wrong direction. My father just said we were going to meet someone. I still had no idea as we pulled into the parking lot at the blimp landing area in Carson, California. After a few minutes my sister and her husband, Joel, pulled up beside us. It was then that she told me about the flight.

We waited a few minutes until the blimp's ground crew was ready for us. They helped Ann, Joel, my parents, and me into the cabin that hangs below the huge blimp. At that time I was still walking, but I needed a boost to get up the ladder. One crewman was in the cabin with a firm hand on my shoulder and another crewman was on the ground pushing on my bottom. I sat in the seat near the front, closest to the door.

We were all surprised at how steeply the blimp lifted off the ground. It went slowly up and forward for about ten or fifteen seconds. Then the nose pointed up and we were rapidly climbing. The roar of the engines increased and we were forced back against our seats. When you see the blimp in the sky, it looks like it is floating lazily, just like a balloon, but from inside, the feeling is completely different. We flew out over the Pacific Ocean and circled south toward the Palos Verdes Peninsula. The cabin has sloping sides and you can look down without leaning over. I'm not fond of heights, but I was very comfortable in my seat. The flight took about forty-five minutes. When it was over, we descended just as steeply as we had climbed. I braced my feet against the floor and was thankful I had on a sturdy seatbelt. There is a municipal golf course next to the landing field and it felt as though we were preparing to strafe the golfers as the nose of the blimp tilted downward. We could see the golfers looking anxiously up at us. At the last moment the blimp leveled off, the ground crew grabbed tether lines hanging from the blimp, and the engines quieted to an idle. Exiting was easier than entering. A crewman inside grabbed my shoulders and a crewman outside grabbed the sides of my leg braces. They picked me up and lowered me to the ground.

In October 1980, I was elected president of the Polio Survivors Association. The Polio Survivors Association was incorporated in 1975 to promote the well-being and improve the quality of life of severely disabled polio survivors. The original intent was to advocate for additional funds to help with personal care and other needs associated with severe disability. Many severely disabled polio survivors had a support structure that included parents and siblings. These parents and siblings were getting older and were not always available to provide the help needed.

An additional goal was to encourage local, severely disabled polio survivors to become more active outside their homes. Many, because of ventilator dependence, had become fearful of leaving the safety of home. We were able to provide transportation that included personnel trained in the intricacies of mechanical ventilation. We sponsored several events each year where polio friends could meet, have fun, and exchange coping skills. Rancho Los Amigos supported our efforts. In fact, Rancho still has a weekly outpatient polio clinic, and is one of the few facilities with this continuity of care for polio survivors.

As the late effects of polio became more of an issue, we began to broaden our efforts to include these new challenges. In 1985, I wrote a "Poliomyelitis Fact Sheet" to provide some basic information about polio. Many of those who contracted polio were infants or young children and had little recollection of their early hospitalization. Our organization gathered other relevant information, which we share with polio survivors and health professionals. Our Web site has a great deal of information about polio and post-polio. We also have a number of photographs that illustrate the polio experience.

Being president of the Polio Survivors Association has brought me in contact with a lot of very interesting people. It has also labeled me as an expert on polio and long-term disability. I do know a lot about these subjects, but I doubt that I'm an expert. Is anyone? Our polio experiences are so diverse, and there are so many different types of disabling conditions, that it would be difficult to be an "expert" on these issues.

I also serve on the board of Rancho's Amigos Fund. The Amigos Fund is Rancho's patient welfare fund. We have been serving the special needs of Rancho's patients since 1954. We provide financial resources for many needs, primarily through revolving funds for the Nursing, Social Work, and Recreation Therapy departments. We can also respond to special requests rapidly and efficiently. Every penny of every dollar we raise goes directly toward patient needs. We have no overhead expenses.

On June 6, 1982, I got an interesting call from Bill Saar, the patient ombudsman at Rancho. He told me that Piper Laurie, the actress, was at Rancho trying to prepare herself for a part in the television mini-series of *The Thorn Birds*. She was to portray an innkeeper's wife, who was described in the novel as "walking with sticks." Most people understood this to mean she had polio. Bill wanted to know if Miss Laurie could come to our house and talk to me. Of course I agreed. Piper Laurie was a delight to meet. She asked questions about the way she should walk and what adaptations she would have to make to portray her character. My mother prepared lunch for us and Miss Laurie stayed for about two hours.

In June 1983, I was asked to serve on the faculty of an international polio conference being held in St. Louis, Missouri. We flew in a Lockheed L1011 from Los Angeles to St. Louis on a Thursday morning and returned the following Monday. This was the first time I had flown on a commercial airliner. I had been up in a small, single-engine plane back in the late 1950s and, as related before, up in the Goodyear blimp in 1980. Now I could boast of being on another means of transportation. My list now included steam and diesel trains, small power boats, a sailboat, an ocean liner, a single-engine aircraft, a commercial airliner, and a blimp. Of course, cars, buses, and trucks too. I haven't been in a helicopter yet, but I'm thinking about it.

It was at the St. Louis conference that the term "post-polio syndrome" first became known. Some mention of the late effects of polio had been printed in earlier medical journals but few people took notice. Now, because thousands of polio survivors from the 1940s and 1950s were beginning to experience this problem, the media began to take an interest. A crew from CBS was there taping a segment to be used on *Sunday Morning with Charles Kuralt*. When it aired a week or two later, I was surprised to see a short glimpse of me in the background entering the main conference room.

About this same time, I was working on a volunteer assignment at Rancho with my friend Justin Laird. He was using his electric wheelchair and I was trying to keep up on foot. As I was walking down the hall, one of the pulmonary staff physicians casually asked how I was doing. I replied that right at the moment I was pooped. Instead of just waving off my comment he stopped and asked additional questions. After a short conversation, he suggested that it might be appropriate for me to start using an electric wheelchair to conserve my strength and energy. He made arrangements with the Physical Therapy Department to have me fitted. After several months, I received my chair. This has allowed me to continue my volunteer activities. Many people with disabilities resist the use of assistive devices. They think they would be "giving in" if they used them. On the contrary, I feel they are very liberating. In fact, I felt just like a kid with a new toy.

Another liberating piece of equipment I bought was a computer. This is one of my greatest aids to communicating. I write letters and do graphics and publishing jobs for several non-profit organizations. I also used it to publish the *Polio Survivors Newsletter* for most of the fourteen years I was the editor, and I still edit the newsletter for the Rancho Los Amigos Post-Polio Support Group. I designed and maintain the Polio Survivors Association Web site (www. polioassociation.org) with my computer, as well as our family Web site (www.downeydaggetts.com).

In 1993, I used the computer to write a comprehensive report on home-based, long-term care, which was later reprinted in the journal of the American Academy of Home Care Physicians. I am a lay member of this medical organization. I don't know how people can function effectively without using a computer. I'm writing this life review on my computer. Since my first computer in 1983, I've traded up to a more powerful unit at least nine times.

The computer is liberating, but it has not been labor or time saving for me. It has certainly helped me to do many things, but that is the problem. Because I can now do them better, I do a lot more of them. During the 50s, 60s, 70s, and into the early 80s, I read voraciously. My reading tastes leaned toward non-fiction, mostly history, biography, etc. I just don't have the time to read as much now. I don't have the energy either. The afternoons were the times when I did most of my reading. Now I devote most afternoons to resting in bed.

 $\mathcal{60}$ $\mathcal{60}$ $\mathcal{60}$ $\mathcal{60}$ $\mathcal{60}$

In the early 1980s, I participated in a group interview conducted by a psychologist who appeared regularly on local television. He asked all of us some rather personal questions. Every time he came around to me he would ask about my relations with other people, if I had considered marriage and, if not, why. I explained some of the disincentives built into our economic and cultural systems that people with severe disabilities must think about before getting married, especially if the spouse is not disabled. A person will almost always lose any government-supported financial assistance and will often lose their medical coverage. I explained that in my case, I could live with a person and as long as I called that person my provider of personal assistance services, or "aide," we could have an adequate income. But if I legally married that same person, our income would be cut almost in half. This applies to employment too. A person would have to find a very lucrative job, or be independently wealthy, to compensate for the loss of income and medical coverage. Medical coverage can be a very big issue for someone with a significant disability. I told him about people I know who have tried both options: marriage and/or employment. A few are successful. Some barely struggle by. Most end up divorced or quit their jobs in frustration. The system often punishes those who try the hardest. My portion of the interview never made it on the air. He appeared to be more interested in the physical relationships of disabled people.

I've never had a physical relationship. I've rationalized this by saying that I didn't want to bring a child into this world without an adequate income to provide for him or her. This might be old-fashioned, but having a wife and children without being able to support them is not acceptable to me. And I've had so many x-rays that any child of mine would probably have two heads.

But, if I'm really honest with myself, it probably has more to do with that pretty low physical self-image I mentioned earlier in this life review. I've tried hard to overcome it, but when I look in the mirror, I still see an image that doesn't even remotely resemble the stereotype of masculinity. Coupled with this is the knowledge that I would need help with most of the basics involved with such a relationship: transportation, getting undressed, etc. This has been even more of a psychological obstacle in recent years. I have a hard time imagining myself saying, "Would you like to go out with me? Oh, by the way, you'll have to come to my house and drive my van. And it would probably be a good idea if you learned to use my suction machine and other life support equipment." In addition, living with my parents certainly hindered my privacy in this area. They would not have objected—they probably would have encouraged me—but the next day I'd probably get the "Where did you go?" and "What did you do?" questions. I know that deep inside of me there has always been a person wanting to enter into an intimate relationship and bond emotionally with another human being. There have been times, especially when I was younger and alone at night, that I would despair of ever expressing those feelings. If I have any major regret in my life, it would be that I was not open to a long-term relationship. And, truthfully, I believe I would have made a good husband and father. I'm not angry with myself, or particularly sad, but I do occasionally have brief episodes of melancholy.

Polio Déjà Vu

The years from the late 1950s to the early 1980s were my best, physically. I walked well, if stiffly, and had a high level of function. I needed help with some tasks but was fairly independent. However, because of reduced pulmonary capacity, I didn't have the energy to work all day, every day. A regular nine-to-five, five-days-a-week job was not possible. This is one reason I volunteer with many organizations. I can pick my hours and tasks.

୧ଦ   ୧ଦ   ୧ଦ   ୧ଦ   ୧ଦ

My left hand was most affected by polio, but the middle finger on that hand had some strength. It could flex and hold weight. I'd use this finger to hook onto a belt loop of my pants as I pulled them up. One morning in the early 1980s, as I sat on the side of the bed getting dressed, I discovered that the finger wouldn't work. This was probably my first noticeable symptom of what we later came to know as post-polio syndrome.

Post-polio syndrome, or the late effects of polio, affects most polio survivors. My problems started thirty years after my initial recovery period. It was almost as if my warranty had run out. I still functioned reasonably well but I noticed a loss of strength, and I was tiring more easily.

My parents and I had season tickets to the Downey Symphony concerts. We always sat in the balcony because we had a better view of the entire orchestra from there. Climbing the stairs had never been a problem. Now, when I reached the top, I'd have to pause a few seconds and catch my breath. At first I thought this was because I was getting older.

     ∾   ∾   ∾   ∾   ∾

Late in June of 1984, I felt as if I was coming down with a cold. With me a cold usually has three stages: several days of congestion and discomfort, three or four days of gradual improvement, and another week to get back to normal. This cold, or whatever it was, just did not respond to my usual treatments. I went to a doctor in our new HMO and he did a very brief examination. He said I was just tired and I should go home and rest. If I had taken his advice I'd probably be dead. I felt miserable, and knew enough about pulmonary issues to realize something wasn't right. I made an appointment to see my friend Elaine Layne, the Nurse Practitioner on the Pulmonary Service at Rancho. She advised me to have my CO_2 level and other blood gasses checked.

Given the way I felt, it didn't surprise me that my CO_2 was elevated. What did surprise me was that it had shot through the roof. My CO_2 had been running between 50 and 55 mm Hg, and this is somewhat higher than the normal 35 to 45 mm Hg. Now it was 80! My blood oxygen level had fallen dangerously too. Obviously, I was not getting adequate ventilation. On July 11, 1984, I once again became a Rancho Los Amigos inpatient.

For two weeks we tried several non-invasive respiratory options. I just couldn't seem to tolerate them. Even using my chest respirator full time didn't seem to help. To compensate for my reduced ventilation I was given oxygen, but I knew this was not a good long-term solution. Administering oxygen will help with blood oxygen levels, but it can mask CO_2 retention, and this can be fatal. After much thought, I decided that another tracheostomy would be the best choice for regaining my pulmonary health.

The prospect of having another trach didn't frighten me. I have several good friends who still function well with trachs after more than thirty years. If our vision is less than perfect, we wear glasses. If our hearing is impaired, we get hearing aids. To me, it was not such a huge leap of faith or logic to get help when my breathing became compromised.

On the other hand, having a trach would mean I couldn't wear a tie. It may sound odd, but this was my only real psychological hurdle. I really enjoyed wearing a suit and tie. I looked better, and I felt my disability was less obvious.

This decision to have a trach was not made in a vacuum. For several years, the doctors had kept a very close watch on my CO_2 levels. This was coupled with a borderline vital capacity of about 1,000 milliliters, approximately 23 percent of normal. Having made the decision, I was sent to surgery on Monday morning, July 30, 1984. I was relieved to learn that this tracheotomy, unlike my original one thirty-one years before, was going to be done under general anesthesia. I didn't look forward to a repeat of my 1953 experience with trach surgery under local anesthesia.

I awoke after surgery with a number 8, cuffed trach. This type of trach has an inflatable "cuff" that closes off a person's airway, above the trach, to prevent any leakage of air through the nose or mouth. It also prevents a person from talking. The doctor explained that he had to remove quite a bit of scar tissue left over from my 1953 trach. It required several stitches to help keep the tissue tight around the opening.

Three days later I was back on the ward, and after two more days the stitches were removed. A size 6 trach with no cuff was put in. Without the cuff, I was able to talk again. The type of respirator I was using had multiple hoses and it was difficult to move without pulling on the trach. This was very, very uncomfortable.

Living close to Rancho, my parents were able to come at least two and sometimes three times a day, usually at mealtimes. This helped quite a bit. Not only did it break the monotony, but they brought in some home-cooked food. Rancho food is good, but, like any institutional food, it can't compare with home cooking.

In the middle of August, the bulky, multi-hosed respirator I was using was replaced by a much smaller, portable, single-hosed positive pressure volume ventilator (PVV). This was a great improvement. I could move much more freely. I was also given some time off the respirator. I was encouraged to sit on the side of the bed and take a few steps. After more than a month in bed, I felt pretty wobbly. The first two or three times, the therapist recommended that I use my respirator as we walked. I found this cumbersome and asked to try walking without it.

To my real relief, I had no trouble making the adjustment, but it took several days before I felt very steady on my feet. I'm sure that the weeks I spent lying in bed had a very debilitating effect. Still, each day I walked a little farther down the hall.

This was the time of the 1984 Los Angeles Summer Olympics, and the television coverage of this event helped to break the monotony. In addition, a segment for the television series *Highway to Heaven* was being filmed right outside my window. This added a little extra diversion.

I was discharged exactly eight weeks after being admitted to Rancho. The new trach and the weeks in bed, coupled with some of the late effects of polio, caused some changes in my life. I couldn't stand in the shower safely, both because of my increased weakness and because of not wanting to get the tracheostomy wet. The trach made it more difficult to cough naturally, but it facilitated mucous management mechanically. I couldn't cough it up very well, but I could suction it out of my airway, if needed.

I reduced my activities to compensate for my lower energy level. I was probably pushing my limits anyway, since for many years I had been very involved with a variety of church, civic, and disability-related organizations. I've tried to be more selective and conserve my energies for those things that I feel are most important. I try, but I'm not always successful. I have a very hard time saying no to projects that I feel are worthwhile.

1985 was the thirtieth anniversary of the Salk polio vaccine. A specially engraved plaque was to be presented to Dr. Jonas Salk at an international polio conference held in St. Louis, similar to the conference I had attended in 1983. Dr. Salk was the man who developed the first effective polio vaccine. He could not be at the conference because of a prior speaking commitment, so the conference organizers asked me to present the plaque to him at the

Salk Institute in La Jolla, California. I talked to Dr. Salk on the telephone several times, and we were able to schedule a time that was convenient for both of us. My father drove me to La Jolla and my mother accompanied us. She was thrilled with the opportunity to meet the man who was most responsible for the first effective polio vaccine.

Jonas Salk was very gracious. He said he was sorry that he hadn't been able to get the vaccine into use in time for me to benefit. He asked about my polio experiences and gave us a tour of the Institute. It was a real pleasure meeting him. When he died in 1995, CBS radio called me to get my reaction to his death. I think I expressed my admiration for him, both as a person and as a medical pioneer. At least I hope I did. I didn't know it, but my telephone conversation was being broadcast live. A friend from church told me later that he was driving down the freeway, listening to the radio, and all of a sudden he heard my voice.

Because I was president of the Polio Survivors Association, and because of my contacts at Rancho, I was asked by CBS News to provide background material on polio for a feature they were doing to mark the polio vaccine anniversary. They came to our house to tape part of a feature that appeared on the *CBS Evening News.* I was also interviewed by most of the local television stations.

One thing that astonished me was the amount of ignorance about polio, even by people who should know better. I met an osteopathic doctor who said that it was impossible for anyone to live more than a few years in an iron lung. He said, "It wasn't natural!" This statement came after I had told him that I personally knew of two people who had been living in tank respirators since 1948. He offered the explanation that *I* must be misinformed! I suggested that he talk to Marjorie Harper, one of our board members, and gave him her telephone number. He could then hear for himself that she was one example of a very alive and vital iron lung resident. He wasn't interested!

Another example that shocked me, although it probably shouldn't have, was an interview with Ed Roberts that appeared on the television program *60 Minutes.* Ed was the director of California's Department of Rehabilitation during the 1970s. He also happened to be a respirator-dependent, quadriplegic, polio survivor. The interviewer was openly shocked when he found out that Ed had married after contracting polio and was the father of two boys. Ed noticed the reaction and explained that polio has no effect on one's reproductive system. I know many severely disabled polio survivors, both men and women, who have become parents. I knew two ladies who gave birth while in the iron lung, and one lady who conceived while in an iron lung. Polio has no effect on the sensory organs either, but many people who should know this apparently don't. I heard one of President Franklin Roosevelt's sons talk about his father's "dead, unfeeling legs." This is nonsense!

I was admitted to Rancho again in March of 1986 with pneumonia. I had a fever of 103 degrees and a great deal of congestion. With medication, the congestion subsided, but I continued to have a low-grade fever for several weeks. It would be close to normal in the mornings but elevate in the afternoons. I was given antibiotics intravenously, and had just about every diagnostic test known to man. I had a bronchoscopy, an echocardiogram, tuberculosis tests, a zillion x-rays, more blood tests than I can count, and several trips to nuclear medicine. Joking with the hospital staff, I told them I had every test except an autopsy and I wasn't ready for that yet. In general I felt pretty good, but the doctors just couldn't figure out why my temperature was so persistent. After five weeks, it returned to normal and I returned home.

Despite my reduced activity level, the years from 1986 through 1989 were very rewarding. I concentrated my efforts on issues relating to Rancho Los Amigos. In 1986, Rancho was beginning to prepare for its centennial celebration in 1988. I was asked by the hospital administration to represent the thousands of polio patients who had been treated at Rancho over the years. I served on the Centennial Committee, and a sub-committee appointed to oversee the publishing of a large, beautifully illustrated centennial book. I also served as chair of the committee to plan the gala, Centennial Banquet.

Because of these activities, I was selected as Rancho's 1988 Volunteer of the Year. The award was presented during a festive luncheon at the Dorothy Chandler Pavilion of the Los Angeles County Music Center. About thirty volunteers were recognized, one from each county department. I also received the 1989 Los Angeles County Distinguished Volunteer Award. This is given, annually, to five individuals out of the county's seventy-thousand plus volunteers. This was a real honor, and a complete surprise.

In conjunction with my Rancho activities, and as part of my duties as president of the Polio Survivors Association, I have authored several pieces of legislation benefiting those with severe disability. My state representatives introduced the bills. Most were successfully passed and signed by the governor. These ventures into the legislative arena brought attention at the state level and resulted in my receiving a resolution from the California State Senate commending my efforts.

In the summer of 1989, I began putting together information for a Daggett family history. I asked my father, his sister, and their surviving brothers to write about their memories of early life. I tried to get my mother to do this too. She made a good start but she never finished. You can read their stories on our family's Web site: www. downeydaggetts.com. I decided to begin writing my own story at the same time, and this life review is a result.

My physical condition continued to deteriorate, which was anticipated but still frustrating. When I could no longer get up the steps into our house, my father built a ramp up to the back door. I could walk up the ramp, and I figured that when the day came when even this might not be possible, I could roll up in my wheelchair. Unfortunately, my increased weakness also meant that I couldn't get up the steps to my friends' houses. I began turning down social invitations. My pulmonary capacity diminished too. Through the 1960s and 70s I had a vital capacity of about 1,000. Now I have to really work to get it up to 650. This means I must spend more time on the respirator.

My reduced stamina means I'm not able to travel either. Actually, I could travel, but the logistics of bringing all my life support stuff is just too complicated. This has been a real disappointment. I'm glad I did so much when I was able. If I ever win a lottery, the first thing I'd do is buy a large motorhome and hire a driver. There are many things associated with our travels that I really miss, like taking a little-used, often unpaved road and photographing wildflowers. Or sitting beside a mountain stream and listening to the water tumbling over the rocks. I also miss trips to the beach and setting up my spotting scope. We still go to our local beaches occasionally, but I'm not able to stand long enough to use the scope to much advantage. Perhaps I'll design a tripod adapter for my wheelchair.

Starting in 1993, and continuing for over a year, I began having a series of aggravating health problems. They weren't life-threatening but, cumulatively, they were very debilitating. For weeks at a time, I'd wake up in the morning feeling bad physically, and this took a toll on me psychologically. Disability, by itself, had never been a problem for me, but not feeling well for long periods of time was getting to me. The unexpected death of my friend Justin Laird from polio-related complications added to my gloom. I decided to get some professional help. I contacted Dr. James Pasino, head clinical psychologist at Rancho. I'd never felt the need for this type of counseling before, but recognized that I was not coping very well. Although I kept up a good front with my family and friends, inwardly I was having a very tough time. Dr. Pasino and I talked several times during 1995. Just having an objective listener was a great help.

No one in my family knew about this. I was not ashamed of seeking professional help, and I think most of them would have understood, but I just didn't feel it was necessary for them to know.

As I finished the paragraph above, it dawned on me that there are probably a number of facets of my life that are unknown to others. Perhaps "unknown" is too strong. This makes it sound like I've led a double life. It would be more accurate to say that I've never had the urge to "spill my guts" or go into detail about my innermost thoughts and feelings. I don't know if this is healthy or not. Perhaps writing this life review is my way of expressing some of this. I've been much more open about personal matters in this version of my story than I have in the versions that I've shared with others. I have never had a problem talking about my life, even personal aspects of my life, but I've only done this if asked. I don't usually offer any of this unsolicited.

For example, one experience that very few people knew about involved the 1971 sex and disability study that I participated in. One of the leaders of this study was a doctor at a fertility clinic. As the study was coming to a close she asked, privately, if I had ever considered being a sperm donor. I told her that it had never crossed my mind. She finally convinced me to donate. I visited her clinic three times, at about two week intervals. They never tell you how the donations are used, or if someone actually conceived, but some time later I got a cryptic note from her. All it said was, "Success." I've occasionally wondered if I had a son or daughter out there in the community.

As I was coming to grips with these physical and psychological problems, a health crisis occurred that had life-altering potential. During a routine health check up I had blood drawn for a PSA test. PSA is short for prostate-specific antigen. This is a screening test for prostate cancer. My test came back at 5.1. This is above the normal range. After a second PSA test to confirm the results, my urologist recommended a biopsy of my prostate. The biopsy was uncomfortable but not very painful. The really stressful part was waiting for the biopsy results. Prostate cancer treatments can cause incontinence and loss of sexual function. Both of these possibilities were hard for me to anticipate. I have enough trouble getting dressed and undressed without worrying about incontinence, and the prospect of losing sexual function posed additional stress. All of my adult life, there have been things that I would like to do—like hiking, woodworking, and gardening—but I knew that my physical limitations made them next to impossible. I was always able to accept this as a fact of life.

On the other hand, I had never participated in a sexual relationship either, but I always knew that if conditions were right I could. Now, even that possibility might be taken away. I had a hard time dealing with this. To my very real relief, the biopsy was negative.

About this same time, it became apparent that we needed more help in our home. My parents were both getting older and experiencing the frailties that often accompany age. While they continued to provide me with the personal care I needed, it was becoming more difficult for them. For several years, we had two ladies come twice a month to do house cleaning, mostly the kitchen and bathroom, with some vacuuming and dusting. This seemed to work for a while, but now more help was needed. I called Nora Pla, a friend who had worked for Justin, to see if she could recommend someone. Nora was working with a lady who had a stroke, but said she might be able to help us part-time. Nora began working for me full-time in 1996.

She came in the mornings about seven, got me dressed, and fixed my breakfast. Nora also did much of the housework. She drove and did a lot of extra things for my parents and me. She was really great with my mother. Her whole family is special. Her mother speaks only Spanish and I speak very little Spanish. She is such a sweet person; it would be nice to be able to communicate better.

Ever since Rancho's Centennial Celebration in 1988, I had worked at getting some positive media coverage for Rancho. I was able to get Channel 7, our local ABC affiliate, to tape a short segment on the pediatrics unit, but most of my efforts did not achieve the results I had hoped for. I arranged for most of the state and federal resolutions to mark this milestone, but I was still disappointed. When Huell Howser began his two series, *Visiting* and *California's Gold* on KCET, our PBS affiliate, I thought that Rancho would be an excellent subject. After more than five years of writing letters, and a personal visit to KCET, he finally agreed to my invitation. He was impressed with Rancho's polio history and the work being done now with spinal cord injury. Huell and his cameraman, Luis Fuerte, came to Rancho on June 19, 1996. They spent the entire day taping interviews with current and former staff and several patients. I was his "co-host" for the show, which was a real treat. His programs are usually half an hour long, but he said he had enough material to make a one-hour special. It turned out well.

Shortly after the Huell Howser program, I was invited to participate in the filming of a documentary on polio. It was to be called *A Paralyzing Fear: The Story of Polio in America*. I had appeared on television before, but this was the first time I was before a real motion picture camera. My portion of the film was shot at a hotel in Santa Monica, California. The producer was the off-camera interviewer, and in the room with us were a cameraman, a lighting man, a soundman, a makeup lady, and a gofer. The gofer would go for this and go for that. His job seemed to be making sure the lens was clean and enough film was in the camera. After editing, my segment lasted only a few seconds, but the film was very good and appeared on PBS.

A year later, I appeared in another polio documentary. This one was called *A Fight to the Finish: Stories of Polio*, and part of it was filmed in our backyard. This documentary put more emphasis on how polio impacted the family unit. My part in this documentary was pretty brief too, but a little longer than in the first film. I enjoyed the whole experience. Like the earlier one, it dealt with polio's history, but it did it on a more human level. My father and my brother Robert also appeared in this film.

I learned during the filming that Robert had been afraid—I think he used the word "panicked"—that he might get polio too. A day or two after my official diagnosis of polio, he had to get an injection of gamma globulin. This gives a boost to the immune system and was the only defense available against a communicable disease.

We had never discussed this. I always had the feeling that he might have felt left out during that time, since everyone was focused on me. I was still at County General, in the Communicable Disease Ward, when his sixteenth birthday came and went. In the 1950s, a sixteenth birthday could be a big thing, especially for a guy. You could get your driver's license! Freedom! Robert said being in the background didn't bother him. He already had a learner's permit to drive. But polio, contagious polio, *that* was scary. He also mentioned coming to visit me after I arrived at Rancho. The room filled with iron lungs, making their unique whooshing sounds, really affected him.

ℭ ℭ ℭ ℭ ℭ

In 1996, my mother began having more trouble getting around, and her mind was not as focused. She was diagnosed with mild dementia. As the year progressed, so did her dementia. She would ask for help to get into bed at night, and then a half hour later she would be sitting on the side of the bed asking once again to go to bed. She would often call my father's name repeatedly. We hired a lady to help my mother, but she resisted help from anyone other than my father.

Then, right after Christmas, our whole household came down with some kind of respiratory bug. We took my mother to the emergency room because of her high fever, but they said there were not enough available beds. If they admitted her, she would have to stay on a gurney in the hallway. We brought her home again. A day later, my father caught the same bug and could hardly stand. Then I caught it. I developed a fever of over 104 degrees and was admitted to Rancho. My mother's continuing fever added to her increasing disability, and we decided that she would not be able to stay at home. It was with extreme reluctance that we had to place her in a nursing facility. My father and I were both too sick to do much about it, so it fell on my sister to do the actual placement, which was especially hard on her.

After my mother entered the nursing facility she became physically weaker, but her mental state improved. We took her to church most Sundays and out to lunch when we could arrange it. I'm sure some people felt she didn't really know or appreciate what went on during church, but quite often after church she would ask where Lydia (her best friend) was, or remark about our organist, "I didn't see Jeremy."

I was in the hospital two weeks, most of that time in bed. After about eight days, my respiratory infection was under control and Dr. Reddy told me I could be discharged. Unfortunately, the prolonged bed rest left me so weak I was unable to walk more than a step or two. I explained this to the doctor, and expressed my very real concern about functioning at home without the ability to walk or even transfer to and from my wheelchair without help. I'd known Dr. Reddy for many years, and she knew my parents and my living arrangements. She agreed to keep me in the hospital a few more days and have a physical therapist work with me to get some strength back in my legs.

She also recommended that I apply for the Medi-Cal (Medicaid) home care program. This program pays for licensed nurses to stay at a disabled person's home. I doubted that I would qualify, either financially or because of my level of function. But, much to my surprise, I was approved for sixteen hours a day, seven days a week. My approval was expedited because of my respirator dependence. On the whole, this has been good, but it required quite a bit of adjustment. I was not used to having someone looking over my shoulder all the time.

I was actually approved for twenty-four hour coverage, but I didn't want to lose Nora. I arranged it so that I could still have Nora in the mornings. She fixes my breakfast, gets me ready to go out, and drives me to meetings and shopping. Now, however, the nurses do most of my personal care. They are thoroughly professional, but I still felt embarrassment when they would help me bathe. It took a while until I felt comfortable with this.

✧   ✧   ✧   ✧   ✧

On July 22, 2002, I had a second prostate biopsy. Ever since my first one in 1995 my PSA had fluctuated, and almost always in an upward trend. I had regular digital rectal exams, and the urologist always said there were no detectable abnormalities. But with my elevated PSA, he recommended another biopsy.

For the first twenty four hours after the biopsy, everything was normal. There was some blood in my urine, but that was expected. The next day everything went wrong. I couldn't urinate! Evidently one or more blood clots had formed and were blocking my urethra. Nora was on vacation in El Salvador, but my weekend aide, Rosa, was with me. I told her I had to go to the Rancho urology clinic, and I had to get there fast. By the time I got to the clinic I felt like I would burst. My blood pressure was extremely high and I was sweating profusely.

I was catheterized and got relief almost immediately. I returned home with the catheter and leg bag.

For the next ten days, I continued to bleed and would pass blood clots periodically. I also got epididymitis, a pretty painful infection. It was pretty disconcerting to look at the collection bag hanging on my leg and see bloody urine day after day. The catheter didn't bother me too much if I stayed in bed, but if I tried to sit in my wheelchair it was very uncomfortable. So, except for trips to the doctor, I stayed in bed for most of two weeks.

After the second day in bed my legs began to get weaker. I needed to use my Hoyer lift to transfer to and from my wheelchair. This is awkward and time consuming. I also had to use a bedpan for those two weeks, something I hadn't done routinely since the 1950s as a patient at County General and Rancho. I couldn't do much about the bedpan, but I could improve on the lift problem. I had a ceiling-mounted lift installed. This type of lift is a lot easier on me and my caregivers. It was very expensive but I know it was a good investment, if for no other reason than my own peace of mind. My legs regained enough strength so that I could get to the toilet, and I haven't needed to use the lift on a regular basis. It's nice to know, however, that it's available any time I need it. And, to my great relief, the biopsy results were good.

I mentioned earlier in this life review that my disability, by itself, didn't pose a psychological burden. The only time I had a brief negative, even scary, emotional jolt was about this same time. I was in bed and tried to reach the TV remote on the table beside me. My shoulder muscles wouldn't cooperate. I had an almost immediate flashback to Friday, July 17, 1953, the first night I was in the Communicable Disease Ward. I could see myself in that small room, struggling to reach across the bed and falling back exhausted.

Increasing weakness doesn't usually bother me, but it does bring episodes of major frustration. I dislike calling a plumber or electrician for a routine household task. I know how to do most of this stuff. I was rewiring table lamps and fixing toasters when I was nine years old. Plumbing is not rocket science either. It just takes strength and agility that I don't possess. I know how to do most carpenter jobs too. And I enjoy these sorts of things. It would have been exciting and challenging to design and personally build my own house. The designing part I've done. It's the building part that stops me.

Losing strength due to polio's late effects has brought other frustrations. I love to cook, but now I need help with almost every aspect of this. I have wonderful help at home, but I cut down on cooking because I dislike asking for help with every little task. I think many polio survivors have the same problem. We were taught to do things ourselves as much as possible and it goes against this early training to ask for help. I'm always preaching to other polio survivors that this is the new reality, but I often fail to heed my own advice.

I should probably clarify a statement that I've made several times in this life review. I've written that, "disability, by itself, didn't pose a psychological burden." The qualifying words are "by itself." The fact of having a disability is no more a burden to me than becoming bald. It is just a fact of life. We are all different. Few people have perfect bodies. Few people have the ability to run a four-minute mile. Having a disability changed my life, but it didn't ruin my life.

On the other hand, I've had some emotional hurdles. Most I've been able to convert, inwardly, from hurdles to frustrations. Others remain stumbling blocks. Some of my hurdles might have been magnified by the fact that I contracted a pretty severe case of polio as an adolescent, at a time in life when most people begin developing social and dating skills. My early teen years were spent in the relative isolation of a hospital. This relative isolation continued through my high school years. I was no longer in a hospital, but I wasn't *in* school or in the *real world* either.

One aspect of my increasing disability that might be considered "positive" is that I have become less bothered by my outward appearance. When I was walking, and had a higher level of function, I worked at minimizing the appearance of disability. Now I use a large power wheelchair. There is no possibility of hiding this, so I don't even try. In a strange way, this has been liberating. I still try to dress well, within the limits of wheelchair use, but that is about as far as my efforts go. The people I care about know what's inside. They know what kind of person I strive to be. This is all that really matters.

⚮　⚮　⚮　⚮　⚮

My parents died in 2003, within three weeks of each other. My mother died on May 27 and my father on June 16. Mom was ninety-six and dad was one hundred and one. If they had lived a few more weeks, they would have celebrated their seventy-fifth wedding anniversary.

I was saddened by their deaths but I couldn't grieve too much. They both had long and event-filled lives and, until the last few years, they both enjoyed good health. My father especially aged well. Even at one hundred and one he got up in the morning, raised the flag, read the newspaper, and worked the crossword puzzle. My dad often said, after he had been retired several years, that one of his goals was to be retired for as many years as he worked for Western Electric. He surpassed his goal. He worked for Western Electric for thirty-six years and was retired for more than forty-one.

⚮　⚮　⚮　⚮　⚮

In February 2005, I had my third prostate biopsy. Compared to the previous two, this one was a piece of cake. There was very little discomfort during the procedure and almost no bleeding after. Unfortunately, the results weren't as good. My urologist looked at the biopsy report and bluntly said, "You have cancer!" Not, "I'm sorry, but …" or "Unfortunately …" He just announced it, as matter of fact as if he told me it was raining outside.

For the next few months, it seemed that every time I went to a doctor, or had more tests done, the prognosis got worse. The radiologist who read the CT scan and the bone scan indicated that cancer had already metastasized to my bladder and pelvis. Even so, I had no outward symptoms and I felt fine physically. Inwardly, I was a wreck. With resignation, I took the test results with me and went back to my urologist. He looked at the films and the other reports and gave a completely different assessment. He ordered more tests, and these pointed to a localized cancer that could be treated effectively.

My urologist started me on one year of Lupron, a testosterone suppressant, and referred me to a radiation oncologist. I started a nine-week, five-day-a-week regimen of intensity-modulated radiation therapy (IMRT). This is external beam radiation, which I elected to use because it is less invasive and more focused. I became fatigued toward the end of my treatments, and had quite a bit of urinary pain. This was anticipated, but it still took its toll. With medication the urinary discomfort was tolerable, but it was months before I started feeling normal again.

When I was first diagnosed with cancer, I felt as if someone had hit me with a club. But I did my research and chose what I felt were the best treatment options for me. It is too soon to know how effective these treatments have been, at least for the long term, but my latest tests have been encouraging. As I write this, I'm feeling good and I'm hopeful. A person shouldn't ask for more than this.

&ʃ &ʃ &ʃ &ʃ &ʃ

On April 29, 2006, I received the prestigious Amistad Award from the Rancho Los Amigos Foundation. This was presented at a gala, black-tie banquet. Approximately four hundred people attended, and I was especially honored to have over thirty of my family and close family friends join me at this very festive event. Previous Amistad honorees include renowned orthopedic surgeon and polio pioneer Jaquelin Perry, M.D., actress Betty White, and Olympic champion Rafer Johnson.

My relationship with Rancho Los Amigos has extended for more than fifty-five years. This institution and its staff have added immensely to my quality of life. It is fitting that I give of my time in return. Whatever talents I can share, and whatever time and effort I put forth, pales in comparison to what Rancho has given me.

Summing Up

Through all the twists and turns my life has taken, whether public or private, I've had the support of my family. My parents always encouraged me in whatever tasks I undertook. Living with them was certainly to my advantage. Not just because they could provide the assistance I needed in daily activities, but because we enjoyed doing so many things together. I know I would not have traveled as much, nor had as wide a spectrum of experiences, if it were not for them. I've also had the support of my brothers and sister and the encouragement of many friends. In this respect I have been blessed.

My parents were responsible for how I dealt with polio. I never heard them say, "Poor Richard," or any other expressions of pity. My father had a positive, no-nonsense attitude. His advice equated to, "OK, you hit a pothole. Now move on." He would sometimes say to me, "Don't say 'I can't do this.' Say you're having difficulty." My mother was a little more protective. After all, she was my mother. But even she expected that I live my life positively.

My parents also expected that I contribute to society in some way. They were active in the community and expected their children to continue this tradition. That's why I volunteer my time. I truly believe we are put on this earth to help one another. I hope I've made a difference. Realistically, I know I can't solve all the world's problems, but if I can help one person, improve the life of one individual, then I am also enriched.

I have been so fortunate. Yes, I had polio, but I contracted this disease in Los Angeles County. The county had the resources and the will to give the best medical care possible. With additional funding from the March of Dimes, the county built Rancho Los Amigos, the largest and most up-to-date treatment facility for respiratory polio patients in the nation. Rancho gave me the finest rehabilitation available and continues to monitor my pulmonary health. I doubt I would be alive today if it weren't for Rancho's timely medical interventions.

During my polio days at Rancho, I saw miracles every day. I knew a boy of twelve who looked perfectly normal, but polio had robbed him of the ability to swallow. He was fed through a tube. Did this deter him from participating in life? Absolutely not. When patients had birthday parties, he would join us for cake and ice cream. He couldn't swallow any of these treats but he would take a bite and then turn around and discretely spit his unswallowed portion into a basin.

I know several women who returned home, despite quadriplegia and respirator dependence, to raise their children and manage their households. Men, women, and children with varying degrees of disability left the hospital and led successful lives.

I continue to see this with Rancho's current patient population. Individuals with catastrophic injuries are able to put their life back together. People who believe they *can't*, learn that they *can*. I've learned that the real miracles are when ordinary people do extraordinary things. And I've learned something else. I've learned that it's not what life holds that counts, it's what you bring to it.

I was asked once by a television reporter what I thought my life might have been like, had I not contracted polio. I replied that people can't, or at least shouldn't, dwell on things that might have been, because no one knows what "might have been." You just do the best you can. You make decisions based on the information you have and the circumstances at the time.

And almost every time I'm interviewed by a reporter, they say something about how "brave" I am. I find this statement embarrassing.

The first time I heard it I didn't know how to respond. It took me by surprise. Now I tell them, as politely as possible, that bravery has nothing to do with it. Bravery is when a person consciously puts their own life in danger to save or protect someone else. People who have a disability have not made a conscious effort to be disabled. It just happened. They still have the desire to live as full a life as possible. Just like everybody else. You don't have to be brave to do this.

Over the past several years, I've received a few letters from polio survivors who are angry. They feel that they were encouraged, even pushed, to go out and make an active life. They feel this is why they are having trouble now. While I certainly sympathize with them, I don't agree with this outlook. I'm not sure I would have done things much differently, even if I'd known about polio's late effects. I'm a richer person for the people I've met and the things I've done.

I've also talked with polio survivors, and others with disabling conditions, who are having a really tough time. They sometimes ask, "Why me?" I think to myself, "Why not you? What makes you so special that you are immune from life's problems?" Of course I don't actually say this to them. Well, sometimes I do. It depends on the person and the circumstances.

I don't believe that "Why me?" has any point. We know that bad things happen sometimes, but it isn't because we did something to deserve it. If a brick falls off a building, and you are underneath it when it falls, you will be hit on the head. God didn't put you in that spot and God didn't drop the brick. Yes, God made all of creation, including gravity, but the God I know doesn't push bricks off buildings.

If you visit someone with a communicable disease you run the risk of contracting that disease, whether you are a physician or a crook. I have a strong belief in God, but not an anthropomorphic God who looks like an old man sitting on a throne. I can't believe in a God who manipulates peoples' lives and events as if we were puppets on a string.

I remember a play I saw in the early years of public television. It was called *Steam Bath,* and the steam bath attendant was supposed to be God. Every few minutes he would walk to the corner of the room and start pulling levers on a giant console. He would say something like, "There's a black Buick going down Highway 9. I think I'll make it miss the curve and go over a cliff." It was an interesting play, but it was bad theology.

If God doesn't micromanage everything that happens, does prayer do any good? My answer is both yes and no. One person, or ten people, or ten thousand people praying for the flood to recede, the earth to stop shaking, or a plague to end will have little effect. But, if these same people are inspired by their prayers to act, then prayer will have worked. They can find ways to prevent, or at least alleviate disasters, and relieve the suffering they cause. Prayer changes people, not things.

Many people say they talk to God in their prayers. This is fine, but I believe the most effective prayers are when we let God talk to us. I believe prayer is a way that we can allow that "still, small voice" within us all to speak. It can calm our fears. It can help us put things in perspective. And it can inspire us to action. In addition, knowing that others are praying for us, or with us, gives us a sense of belonging to something that is greater than ourselves.

I believe in a God who is with us at all times. You say you can't see Him? I say you see Him every day, working through ordinary human beings. He comes to us in the incarnation of caring people. Friends who support us and uplift us. I believe this because I have seen it and experienced it. We are His instruments on earth. That's the way He works. He sent His Son, fully human, to earth as our guide and teacher. He could have made a wind blow across the land, obliterating illness, famine, and hate, but He gave *us* that responsibility. We haven't done a very good job of it, but that shouldn't stop us from trying.

My faith has led me to become a lay speaker in our local United Methodist congregation. Public speaking is not my greatest gift because, like many respirator users, I sometimes talk in sentence fragments. Still, I feel I have a story to tell. A story that needs to be told. God has blessed my life in more ways than I can count, and His hand has been on my shoulder from my very first day. I'm guessing that there might be some people who cannot understand this statement. All they see is a man in a wheelchair, breathing with the aid of a machine. I hope my talks will change their minds, or at least open their minds to the overwhelming goodness of life. Life is good! God is good! And His love and joy are everlasting!

ہ   ہ   ہ   ہ   ہ

Having had a severe case of polio might have given me a unique insight into the human condition. It certainly made me more sympathetic to the everyday struggles faced by most people. Did polio make me a better person? I hope not. I would like to think that I would have been a good person, no matter what my life experiences included.

In the movie *Saving Private Ryan,* Ryan, as an old man, kneels at the grave of Captain Miller, the man portrayed in the movie by Tom Hanks. He is overcome by emotion. He asks his wife to confirm that he has been a "good man," and thus worthy of Miller's sacrifice. Many people worked to ensure my recovery from polio. I hope that at the end of my life I will be found worthy of their efforts. I hope it will be recorded that I was a "good man."

ہ   ہ   ہ   ہ   ہ

So far I've had a very interesting life. It's been different, but everyone's life is different. I guess, just as in Robert Frost's poem, "Two roads diverged in a wood, and I, I took the one less traveled by …"

There are many things I haven't done that I would like to have done. I would love to walk the entire length of the John Muir Trail, or just once more sing in a mixed chorus or play a saxophone. On the other hand, I've done many things that others only dream about. Saying this, I will close with "To Be Continued."

Above: Richard in 1942, with his brothers, sister, and mother
Below: Richard in 1943, in an old tire swing at Lake Arrowhead

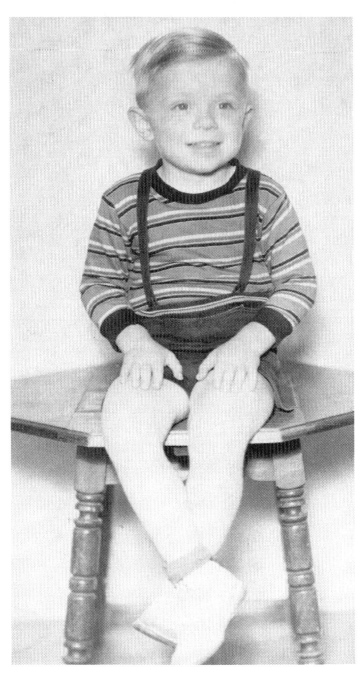

Richard in 1945

Above: The Daggett kids on the porch of their house in Los Angeles. Photograph taken in 1946. Richard's father and grandfather built this house in 1932.
Below: Robert, Richard, Ann, and Rodney Jr. in 1948

Above: Richard's parents in 1948
Below: Richard's parents in 1988

Above: First camping trailer entering Zion National Park in 1946
Below: Second camping trailer in McArthur-Burney Falls
Memorial State Park, California. Both of these trailers were built
by Richard's father.

Above: 109th Street School
(a.k.a. McKinley Avenue School) in Los Angeles
Below: Gallatin School in Downey

Above: Richard in 1952
Below: Seventh Grade band at North Junior High

Above: April 1953. Last photograph of Richard before polio
Below: A polio patient being transferred from the Communicable
Disease building (in the background) to Rancho Los Amigos.
This photograph was taken in 1949. A similar convoy transported
Richard in 1953. Polio patients went to the Communicable
Disease building for the first three weeks of their disease. After
patients were no longer contagious, they were transferred to other
facilities for rehabilitation. If they had significant pulmonary
impairment, as Richard did, they were usually transferred to
Rancho Los Amigos Hospital.

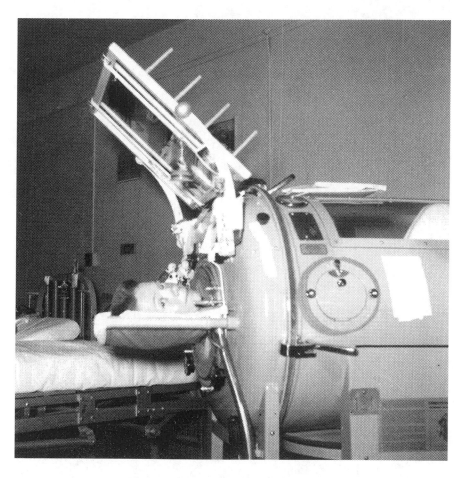

Above: Richard in Building 60 at
Rancho Los Amigos. Photograph taken in September 1953.

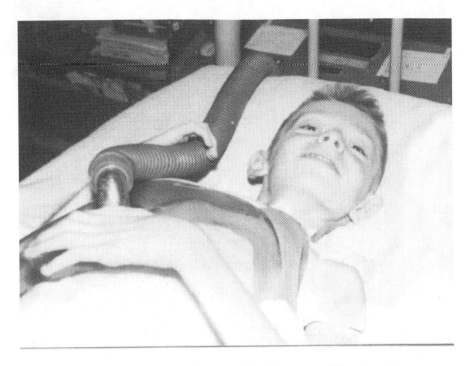

Above: Richard on bed, transitioning out of the iron lung,
using a chest respirator
Below: Richard's first trip home from the hospital, December 1953

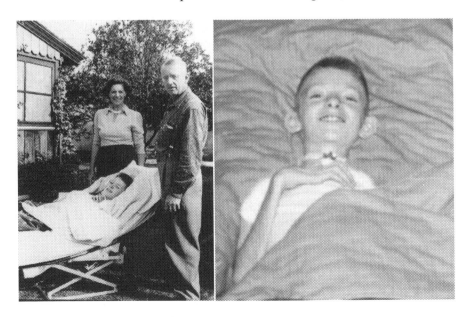

Above: The new 500 Building at Rancho Los Amigos,
shortly after it opened in March 1954
Below: The new 500 Building lobby

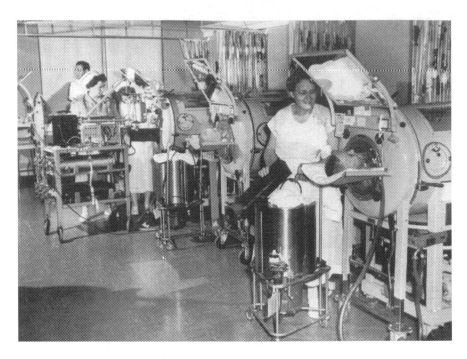

Above: A typical room on the children's unit, Ward 503
Below: Patients moved to Rancho's large auditorium
for a March of Dimes documentary

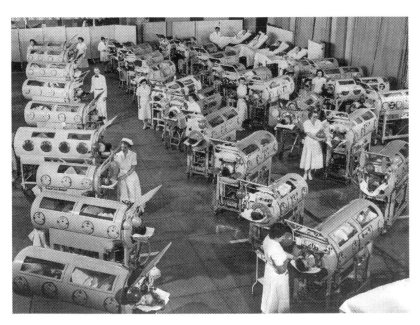

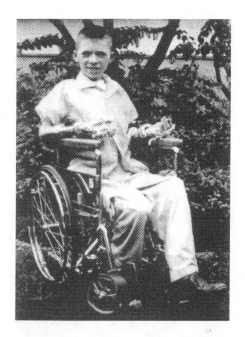

Above: Richard in wheelchair and wearing metal hand splints.
At home for the weekend in 1954.
Below: February 1955. Richard is playing table skittles, a game
presented to him by the British Consul-General. If you look closely,
you can see the scar left from his original tracheostomy and, just
below that, one of the buckles on his plaster body jacket.

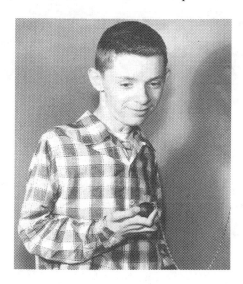

Above: Summer 1955. If you can walk, you can do yard work.
Below: 1955 Chevy and travel trailer at Snow Valley, Idaho

Above: 1959 graduation from Earl Warren High School

Above: 1962 Buick and Airstream "Land Yacht"
on the Blue Ridge Parkway
Below: 400 Airstream trailers in Jasper National Park,
Alberta, Canada

Above left: With "mutton chops" in 1977
Above right: With handlebar mustache in 1978
Below: Richard's parents' 50th Anniversary in June 1978

Above: Wearing three-piece suit in 1984,
a month before second tracheostomy
Below: Richard with Dr. Jonas Salk in 1985

Above: Richard's parents' 60th anniversary in 1988
Below: Richard and Dr. Jacquelin Perry in 1998

Thank you for reading my story. If you have any questions or comments, I'd enjoy hearing from you. I can be reached through:
Polio Survivors Association
12720 La Reina Avenue
Downey, CA 90242
Richard@polioassociation.org

Just What Is Polio And Post-Polio Syndrome?

Poliomyelitis is caused by a virus. It is a highly contagious disease. Polio's effect on the body is commonly classified in these four categories:

- Inapparent or Asymptomatic Carrier: The virus is in your system but it has not affected your own body. You can still pass it on to others.

- Abortive: The word abortive means "tending to cut short." Abortive polio is still polio, but it was "cut short" before it could be detected. There may have been some unrecognized neuromuscular damage.

- Non-Paralytic: The non-paralytic form of poliomyelitis is usually indicated by nausea, headache, sore throat, back and neck stiffness, and pain. In addition, there are changes in reflexes and an elevated spinal fluid cell count. But these are only identified if someone suspects polio and does specific tests. If a person is misdiagnosed as having the flu or summer grippe, then it is unlikely their reflexes or spinal fluid will be checked.

- Paralytic: Acute onset of a flaccid paralysis of one or more muscle groups, without other apparent cause, and without sensory or cognitive loss. Paralytic poliomyelitis is commonly classified in the following sub-sets:

  - Spinal: This type is most frequent and is associated with involvement of the trunk or extremities, more often the lower extremities. Weakness does not fit any pattern.
  - Bulbar: Symptoms can include difficulty in swallowing, loss of voice quality, and sometimes tongue and facial paralysis.
  - Bulbospinal: This type of involvement is usually severe and is associated with respiratory impairment. Between 10 and 25 percent of the paralytic cases seen during the polio epidemics were of the bulbar or bulbospinal type.

The polio virus affects the body by attacking the central nervous system, specifically the anterior horn cells. These motor neurons are located in the front part of the spinal cord and are essential for any muscle activity.

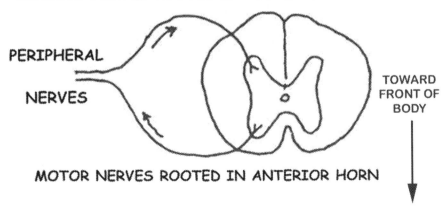

SENSORY NERVES ROOTED IN POSTERIOR HORN

PERIPHERAL

NERVES

TOWARD FRONT OF BODY

MOTOR NERVES ROOTED IN ANTERIOR HORN

The simplified diagram above shows a cross section of the spinal cord. The motor neurons rooted in the anterior horn travel outward through the peripheral nerves to innervate muscle fibers. Depending on the location of the muscles they supply, these motor neurons can be a few inches or several feet long. Sensory nerves travel from their specialized receptors to the spinal cord and enter the posterior horn. Sensory nerves are not affected by the polio virus.

Many individuals lose considerable function during the acute stage of polio but regain a large part of that function during recovery. A significant percentage of these individuals later experience renewed weakness, sometimes accompanied by fatigue or pain. The best medical evidence at this time indicates that a combination of factors associated with overuse is responsible.

If we take a closer look at the recovery process, we can see why this is so. The polio virus attacks randomly. Sometimes motor neuron damage is not severe and the cells can recover much of their function. Other neurons may sustain more complete and irreversible damage. Even if this is the case, it is possible that some function can be restored by "sprouting." Motor neuron cells have the ability to send out new axons. These can innervate neighboring muscle fibers whose own neurons have been destroyed. Motor neurons normally innervate between two hundred and five hundred individual muscle fibers. If a percentage of motor neurons are destroyed, and sprouting takes place, the remaining motor neurons may be innervating as much as four times the normal amount of muscle fiber. The additional load that this places on motor neuron metabolism will cause a failure of impulse strength years later. This seems to begin about twenty to thirty years after polio onset and is probably a contributing factor for the renewal of weakness.

Another possible cause for this renewed weakness, especially in older individuals, is the normal loss of motor neurons. This is a natural part of aging. It is estimated that a person will begin to lose about 1 percent of his or her motor neurons per year after the age of sixty. This is not very significant if an individual starts with 100 percent of their motor neurons, and all of these motor neurons are intact and undamaged. Unfortunately, this is not the case with many older polio survivors. Their supply was depleted by the polio virus and this gradual loss will have a much greater impact.

Some individuals may have gained a degree of recovery by building up the strength of their remaining muscles by exercise and intense use, similar to athletic training. These individuals used this strength in their day-to-day activities and, thus, the muscles have been performing continually at a level that is no longer tolerated.

In addition, many affected muscles that were believed to be "good" or "normal" with manual muscle testing, have been found to be less than this when electromyography (EMG) and other studies were done. In normal activities, these muscles have also been working harder than was once believed.

Muscle weakness due to polio is often asymmetrical. This can put added stress on the entire neuromusclular system, as well as adding strain to joints and supporting ligaments. The result may be an increase in arthritis-like pain.

The question now arises: what can be done to alleviate this condition or prevent the further degradation of muscle strength?

First, polio survivors should seek medical advice to rule out other possible causes for their symptoms. Just because you had polio, this does not make you immune from other physical ailments. Second, it is highly recommended that a complete physical evaluation be done. This should include examination by an orthopedic specialist and complete pulmonary function tests. Ideally, these should be done by physicians who are familiar with polio. You should ask for these test results in writing. Even if no immediate problem exists, this will provide a baseline for measuring your future status.

Lifestyle modification is the most important therapy for new weakness. This will reduce the strain placed on the body. Learning to listen to the body's signals is vital to any plan designed to reduce further degradation of muscle strength. If you're tired, rest. If you hurt, stop. They used to say, "Use it or lose it!" Now we often say, "Conserve it to preserve it!"

Many individuals have asked about the role of exercise for those experiencing the late effects of polio. There have been studies that indicate a 10 percent increase in muscle strength following closely monitored exercise programs. If a person feels they may benefit from additional exercise, then an aerobic type of exercise is probably best.

A twenty-minute program consisting of two to three minutes of activity followed by a minute of rest could be tried. If this makes you feel better continue but, if pain or fatigue results, reduce the exercise until you find a level that can be tolerated. Stopping completely may be best for some. A significant percentage of polio survivors get all the exercise they can tolerate in their activities of daily living. And if it is true that overuse is a contributing cause of renewed muscle weakness, then strenuous exercise regimens should be approached with caution.

An orthopedic specialist may recommend braces, or other assistive devices, to help relieve the stress that is being placed upon weakened muscles and joints. In some cases, this is sufficient to halt the progression of weakness. Selective surgery can sometimes redistribute the residual control so that strain is reduced.

Using assistive devices, such as electric wheelchairs, scooters, etc., is resisted by some individuals. They feel that they are "giving in" to their new symptoms. What they assume to be a burden can actually be very liberating. Using these aids will allow them to conserve their energy for those activities that they feel are most important.

Because pulmonary function has such an important bearing on an individual's general health, this area deserves special emphasis. Standard tables for vital capacities list variables for age and height. These may not have much relevance for many polio survivors. Actual volume, measured in liters or milliliters, is a better indicator of pulmonary status. This test, usually done with a spirometer, is simple and non-invasive. It is a good idea to have your vital capacity measured lying down as well as sitting. For anyone with a volume of less than two liters, a follow-up should be made at least yearly.

Arterial blood gas measurements for CO_2 may be warranted. Generally, CO_2 levels between 35 mm Hg and 45 mm Hg are considered normal. The CO_2 level in your blood can become elevated gradually, without one being aware of the change. If the level becomes high enough, the blood's ability to carry oxygen will be impaired. This could result in headaches or interrupted sleep patterns and may be an indicator of respiratory insufficiency. Respiratory function can also be affected by scoliosis or a reduction in rib cage flexibility that often occurs as a person ages.

The United States Department of Health estimates that there are at least 640,000 polio survivors in the United Sates. Although a significant percentage of these polio survivors are experiencing some late effects, there is no reason to expect that all individuals will be affected. If you would like more information on this and related topics, I recommend you read the various publications of Post-Polio Health International. Inquiries relating to these publications should be directed to Post-Polio Health International at 4207 Lindell Blvd., #110, St. Louis, MO 63108. Telephone (314) 534-0475.

How Many Polio Survivors Are There?

I am sometimes asked the question, "How many polio survivors are there?" That's a good question. I can site various government surveys, and can quote from published articles, but I've always had a suspicion that we are actually underreported.

The following paragraphs in italics are from the Centers for Disease Control (CDC), which is part of the United States Department of Health and Human Services. I have added my related comments at the end of each paragraph.

"Up to 95% of all polio infections are inapparent or asymptomatic. Estimates of the ratio of inapparent to paralytic illness vary from 50:1 to 1,000:1 (usually 200:1). Infected persons without symptoms shed virus in the stool and are able to transmit the virus to others."

Let's use the CDC figure of 200:1. If I read this paragraph correctly, it means that for every person who contracted polio, and had some degree of identified neurologic deficits, there were about two hundred additional people who were infected with the polio virus but nobody knew it.

"Approximately 4%–8% of polio infections consist of a minor, nonspecific illness without clinical or laboratory evidence of central nervous system invasion. This clinical presentation is known as abortive poliomyelitis, and is characterized by complete recovery in less than a week. Three syndromes observed with this form of

poliovirus infection are upper respiratory tract infection (sore throat and fever), gastrointestinal disturbances (nausea, vomiting, abdominal pain, constipation or, rarely, diarrhea), and influenza-like illness. These syndromes are indistinguishable from other viral illnesses."

This paragraph complicates the issue. If there is no *"clinical or laboratory evidence of central nervous system invasion,"* how do we know the person had polio? Did they do a stool culture looking for the polio virus or do a spinal tap? My guess is that doctors wouldn't have done these tests without some evidence of "flaccid paralysis." All the literature I've read says a presentation of flaccid paralysis is the clue that someone has a neuromuscular disease, i.e., polio, West Nile encephalitis, etc.

Of course, if a community was in the midst of a polio epidemic, some of these tests might have been done to any patients who looked as if they might have polio. Polio was very frightening to parents, families, and community health professionals. But even in these circumstances, it is doubtful that every person who complained of *"influenza-like illness"* would be tested.

"Nonparalytic aseptic meningitis (symptoms of stiffness of the neck, back, and/or legs), usually following several days after a prodrome (definition: an early symptom indicating the onset of an attack or a disease) *similar to that of minor illness, occurs in 1%–2% of polio infections. Increased or abnormal sensations can also occur. Typically these symptoms will last from 2 to 10 days, followed by complete recovery. Fewer than 1% of all polio infections result in flaccid paralysis* (definition: weakness or loss of muscle tone resulting from injury or disease of the nerves innervating the muscles)."

The CDC says that, *"fewer than 1% of all polio infections result in flaccid paralysis."* But I've read studies done in the late 1940s by David Bodian, MD, PhD, a distinguished anatomist, that indicate at least 50 percent of motor neurons have to be impaired by the polio virus before there is any visibly apparent paralysis. So, if this is true, then many people probably had polio-related neuromuscular damage without the person, or the medical community, being aware of it. And, if the person had had neuromuscular damage years ago, it seems logical that this would put him or her at greater risk for something like post-polio syndrome.

Does this make it any easier to answer the question? I doubt it. It just illustrates the problem of establishing statistically supportable numbers. Even stating the actual number of "identified" polio survivors is difficult. I've read various medical articles that put the numbers as low as 250,000 and as high as 1,000,000 or more. The 250,000 number is compiled from actual hospital admissions and confirmed diagnosis of at-home polio patients. The higher numbers are estimated from these patients plus national interviews about health issues.

Even if we take the lowest estimate of 250,000 identified polio survivors in the U.S., and agree with the CDC that these people represent just 5 percent of the people who had a polio infection, then there must be at least five million people in the U.S. who were infected. How many of these 5,000,000 people are at risk now of polio-accelerated neurologic damage?

I guess the final question is, can these 5,000,000 people be classified as polio survivors? And, if they are classified as polio survivors, would this trivialize the experiences of those of us who spent weeks or months in hospitals and rehabilitation facilities?

It probably isn't trivial if a person is experiencing the late effects of polio, and they or their doctors have no clue as to the cause. They have no idea that these new problems are being caused by a virus that damaged their neuromuscular system decades before.

Polio Resources

Polio Survivors Association
12720 La Reina Avenue
Downey, California 90242
(562) 862-4508 voice and fax
Web site: www.polioassociation.org
>   *Information on polio and the late effects of polio.*
>   *An excellent resource for students, with descriptive text and*
>   *numerous photographs.*

Post-Polio Health International
4207 Lindell Blvd., #110
St. Louis, Missouri 63108
(314) 534-0475
Website: www.post-polio.org
>   *Information on polio and the late effects of polio.*
>   *Resource list of physicians, other healthcare professionals,*
>   *and polio support groups*

Other important organizations in my life:

The Amigos Fund
of Rancho Los Amigos National Rehabilitation Center
P.O. Box 2370
Downey, California 90242
Web site: www.rancho.org

Downey United Methodist Church
10801 Downey Avenue
Downey, California 90241
(562) 861-9777
Website: DowneyUMC.com